YOUTH SERVICES

Parenting a
Child with Diabetes

D1125059

Other books by Gloria Loring:
Kids, Food, and Diabetes

Parenting a Child *with* Diabetes

SECOND EDITION

A PRACTICAL, EMPATHETIC GUIDE TO HELP
YOU AND YOUR CHILD LIVE WITH DIABETES

Gloria Loring

Foreword by Robert Rood, M.D.

LOWELL HOUSE

LOS ANGELES

NTC/Contemporary Publishing Group

Library of Congress Cataloging-in-Publication Data
Loring, Gloria.
    Parenting a diabetic child : a practical, empathetic
guide to help you and your child live with diabetes /
Gloria Loring
      p.   cm.
    Includes bibliographical references and index.
    ISBN 1-56565-001-8
    ISBN 0-7373-0301-8 (2nd edition)
    1. Diabetes in children—Popular works.
    2. Diabetes in children—Patients—Home care.
    I. Title.
    RJ420.D5L68   1993
    618.92′462—dc20   92-35925
                                                CIP

Text Design: S. Pomeroy

Published by Lowell House
A division of NTC/Contemporary Publishing Group, Inc.
4255 West Touhy Avenue, Lincolnwood (Chicago), Illinois 60646-1975 U.S.A.
Printed in the United States of America
International Standard Book Number: 0-7373-0301-8
99 00 01 02 03 04 VP 18 17 16 15 14 13 12 11 10 9 8 7 6 5 4 3 2 1

This book is dedicated to all of the extraordinary parents who work so
hard for the Juvenile Diabetes Foundation International.

You will notice that, through most of the book, I have almost always referred to the anonymous "child with diabetes" with the pronoun "he." This is not prejudice on my part. I merely found it cleaner and easier reading to use one consistent gender rather than switching back and forth or using "he or she." In an effort to balance that choice, I have referred to all the authority figures as "she."

Contents

Foreword

For over twenty years I have seen thousands of children and their parents come to my office frozen into immobility, afraid to help themselves, unable to take charge of their world. As the senior medical director of the Diabetes Treatment Center in Los Angeles, my role in these first contacts is not to educate but to stabilize these families so they will open their minds and be prepared to learn new and innovative skills to better help their children. Frequently, after I have worked long and diligently with parents, they will look at me with a cold stare and make some variation on the same remark: "How do you really know what we are experiencing, what pain our child is suffering? You're not a diabetic and all the things you have learned have come from books." No degree of protestation on my part, no recital of articles read or written, will give these parents any peace or solace.

They want to hear the "real stuff" from someone who has been there. Someone who has wrestled with her fear and trepidation. A person who has cried herself to sleep at night worrying about what the morning will bring. Gloria Loring has lived that life, has fought those battles, and has had the strength to rise above the emotional fears to ask the most difficult questions: Why are we doing this to my child? What is it supposed to accomplish? Has it worked for others, and where can I reach out to those others for confirmation and support?

I am Brennan's doctor. A doctor is a teacher, a participant, not "God." When Brennan was younger my role was to work with Gloria. She, in turn, translated the information into a practical day-by-day lifestyle for her son. As Brennan grew older he became a co-partner with Gloria, and now that he has entered into the third part of his adolescent development it is imperative that he take his learned and observed experiences and make them his. His task is to assimilate them and create a new and specific blend of strengths and qualities that are uniquely Brennan. As a guide I help navigate this precious cargo from helplessness, through helpfulness. From inquisitive child to competent adult.

Gloria has learned what works and explains it here in terms that are readable and understandable. She has become an ex-officio partner in our medical practice, working with new patients and their families. While I am the physician and look at the issues from the standpoint of medicine, Gloria brings together medical teachings and the warmth and compassion of someone who has lived through a frightening experience and has come out a winner.

This unique combination she also brings to her book, a must-read for any parent of a diabetic child. In fact, I plan to give *Parenting a Child with Diabetes* to all of my patients and their families.

ROBERT ROOD, M.D.
Diabetes Treatment Center
Los Angeles

An Unexpected Gift

Whenever I meet another parent of a diabetic child, I find myself swapping stories about when and how our children were diagnosed. It is comforting to know that someone else has also made it through the tough times. The stories usually end in some negative statement about diabetes. There's certainly a downside to diabetes, but I have seen that there's another facet to this challenge that has entered Brennan's and my life.

In many ways, my son's diabetes has been a gift to me. I know that sounds like a strange thing to say, but it's true. It has altered the course of my life for the better. At the time of his diagnosis, I could not have imagined I would ever feel this way, but time has given me perspective.

From the moment of Brennan's diagnosis, I felt a powerful sense of loss. I had always been very frightened of losing anything or anyone in my life. Yet loss is an essential, natural part of our lives. From the moment we are born, letting go fills our years. We let go of our childhood, our parents, our dreams of omnipotence. We become parents and, once again, begin a cycle of separation. As mothers, we give birth and relinquish our physical connection to our babies. As our children grow, we see that maybe we cannot keep them safe from every harm. Yet we hold on to the illusion that we have some control, thinking that we will always be able to "make it all better."

And perhaps a day comes when we cannot do that. The day I was told my son had diabetes was just such a day. And then comes the anger. Why my child? The guilt. Why didn't I . . . ? And the sadness. It's not right, it's not fair. Please, God, make this go away.

It does not go away. As I write this, it is all there again, that terrible hurt that there is something "wrong" with my son that I cannot fix. So many years have gone by, yet it wells up so easily. I ache for him. Even now, there are times I cannot watch him stick that needle into his skin.

So how can this possibly be a gift? Why is it that I will do everything I can to take diabetes out of my son's life, yet I am not so anxious to have it taken from mine? Because it has given my life a larger purpose—finding a cure for my son and all the other people whose lives include diabetes. I would not for a moment wish to go back to being who I was before I had that larger purpose, before diabetes entered my life.

The shift from devastated parent to diabetes advocate began when my friend Valerie Harper provided me with a context within which to view Brennan's diabetes. She had been involved with a hunger organization that believes that ending world hunger by the year 2000 is possible if the political will and commitment can be generated. After Brennan's diagnosis she said to me, "If we can end hunger in twenty years, we can cure diabetes in ten." By saying "we," she inspired me to take on curing diabetes as my personal responsibility.

In 1980, one year after Brennan's diagnosis, I began to do just that when I joined the cast of *Days of Our Lives*. *Days* not only gave me my first acting job, it also gave me an idea for raising money for diabetes research. I noticed that the actors traded recipes in the makeup room while getting ready for the show. It dawned on me that a celebrity cookbook could raise money for research. In 1981, after much hard work and many setbacks, I published the *Days of Our Lives Celebrity Cookbook, Volume I.* It was enormously successful. Then in 1983, the *Days of Our Lives Celebrity Cookbook, Volume II* was released. Those two projects, plus an album called "Shot in the Dark" that I produced and recorded as a Juvenile Diabetes Foundation International fund-raiser, raised almost $1 million for diabetes research.

I had never been comfortable with asking for what I needed and yet I secured financing to set up a publishing company and a record label, arranged for advertising and publicity to be donated, and got almost everyone to volunteer their time. I was able to do it because I was asking for help to find a cure for my son. Since then, I have been able to take that same persistence and commitment and apply it successfully to all the other areas of my life.

Someone asked me recently if I thought my relationship with Brennan is different because of his diabetes. I have nothing to compare it to since it's the only relationship with him that I have, but I know I am a more conscientious mother than before. I have learned to let go of some of my controlling ways (and I'm working on the others!). I used to get upset when little things went wrong. Not anymore. Most all problems seem very small compared to having your child's life in jeopardy. I now know that I have the right to ask for what I need in life. I'm no longer frightened by loss. I accept as truth that old saying, "God does not close one door without opening another." The loss I experienced when Brennan was diagnosed has been replaced by my resolution to cure his diabetes.

Yes, Brennan's diabetes has been a gift to me: a gift that changed my life, turning me from a woman who accepted what life threw at her to one who understands that any one of us can move mountains when she is willing to invest her heart and her mind. I have seen my life expanded and enriched by my association with JDF. I have come to know and love an extraordinary group of dedicated men and women at JDF who constantly serve as my role models. I have formed businesses to raise funds for research. I've written books to reach out to other parents. I have learned to be a spokesperson for diabetes research. I have traveled extensively, giving concerts for JDF, and testifying before Congress.

I have had the chance to do things I never would have done otherwise. You might think all this is only because I hold some privileged position as an entertainer, but I have seen so-called "ordinary" men and women accomplish far greater things in the quest to cure their children of diabetes.

I do not regret that diabetes is part of my life. The sadness of my son's diagnosis still exists, but it is wedded to the promise we at JDF have made to our loved ones: "There's a cure and we'll find it." That will be the greatest gift of all!

Acknowledgments

My thanks and appreciation to:

My sons, Brennan and Robin, for their love and support.

My editor, Janice Gallagher, for being so strict.

My friend, Beth, for active listening and good notes.

All the parents who answered my questions so fully and whose remarks are so frequently quoted in these pages.

The Sugarfree Center and Linda Romero Naney for time and advice freely given.

Drs. Sherman Holvey, Jonathan Kellerman, Robert Clemons, Julio Santiago and his team members Susan Greene Davis, Jeanne Bubb, and Debra Kahn, and Paul Madden for sharing their expertise with me.

All the Juvenile Diabetes Foundation International family who share my commitment to find a cure.

In particular, I'd like to thank the two diabetes experts who acted as consultants for this book: Mary Ann Robnett, R.N., M.S., a clinical nurse specialist for the Endocrine/Metabolic Department at Children's Hospital,

Los Angeles, who has worked with diabetic children since 1987, and Robert Rood, M.D., a specialist in diabetes and adolescent medicine for over twenty-five years who is on the Board of Directors for the Diabetes Treatment Centers of America and a past chapter president of the ADA.

From Then to Now

It has been almost twenty fascinating and productive years since my son, Brennan, was diagnosed with diabetes. Years that led to this book, a book filled with all I have learned about parenting a child who has diabetes. I have much to share with you—information and wisdom collected from the many experts who contributed to this book. But first, here is how I came to know about diabetes.

DIAGNOSIS

It happened toward the end of July, 1979. We were on a plane to Canada. My first husband, Alan, had planned ten days of visits with his relatives and we were taking our two sons, Brennan, 4½, and Robin, 2. We began our trip by renting a camper and driving to Kirkland Lake, four hundred miles north of Toronto.

During that trip I noticed a number of changes in Brennan. One afternoon he didn't bother to close the bathroom door in the camper. I watched in amazement as he urinated. The stream that left his body had the force of a fire hose. It was so strong he had to stand back at least a foot from the toilet. His great-grandfather, Will, asked me if I'd noticed how thirsty Brennan was. I hadn't really noticed anything unusual, but then it was summer and very hot and humid. I assumed the heat had made him thirsty, which in turn made him urinate so forcefully.

He was also being very fussy and cranky. It seemed to me there was some correlation between these moods and his having recently eaten ice cream or other sugary foods. I made a mental note to discuss a possible sugar sensitivity with his doctor.

The next day, as Brennan was getting out of the bathtub at his great-grandparents' house, I asked him to step on the scale. The reading shocked me. Six weeks earlier, Brennan had had chicken pox, and I had taken him to the doctor. At that time he had weighed 51 pounds. Yet the scale before me read 46 pounds. How could he have lost 5 pounds? I decided the scale must be off.

About this time the bed-wetting began. Three mornings in a row, Brennan awoke to find his mattress soaked. I told him not to worry about it. There seemed to be good reasons why that might happen. He had been drinking too many liquids, plus we'd been staying up late and he was overtired.

After Kirkland Lake, we drove to Toronto to see Brennan's grandparents. That first night I was watching Brennan go through another one of his cranky fits. Thinking about all the changes going on with him lately, I turned to my father-in-law, a doctor, and said, "I think Brennan has lost 5 pounds. Is that all right?" "He's just losing his baby fat," he said. "That happens to kids his age." I put my concerns aside.

The next day we were on our way to the family reunion. As we approached the campground, I turned to check on the boys in the back of the camper. Robin had fallen asleep. Brennan was staring straight ahead. Suddenly I saw my son clearly, my vision no longer clouded by the excuses of the heat, the hurry of the trip, or the summer thirst. His face was dry and flushed. His eyes were glassy. He stared as if hypnotized, his face devoid of animation. He had no fever, none of the usual signs of illness, but he definitely looked sick. Something was not right, even though we couldn't name it. We made the decision to take him to the doctor as soon as we got home.

We checked in at the campground and spent the day visiting with long-lost relatives. That night Brennan shared the room adjacent to ours with a cousin his own age. As I tucked him in, he asked for a glass of water. He drank it down swiftly. "More, Mommy." He downed the second glass just as quickly. "More." I began to protest, but the urgency of his request stopped me. I brought him a third glass, which disappeared down his throat. I was stunned. I turned to Maxine, the mother of the boy in the other bed who I knew was a nurse. "What would possibly cause a child to drink that much water?"

"There's only one thing I know of," she replied, "diabetes."

There was a name for what was happening to Brennan. Diabetes. I knew nothing about it except that it was a serious illness. The word filled my head as I walked down the hall to the hospitality suite. I found my husband. "Maxine thinks Brennan may have dia . . . . " I was trying so hard to be calm, but each attempt to say the word *diabetes* came out as a sob.

We located a phone and called Brennan's pediatrician back in Los Angeles. I told him about the three glasses of water. He asked if Brennan had been eating a lot. I said I didn't think so. He explained that children with diabetes will eat more than usual but start losing weight. Losing weight? "I think Brennan's lost 4 or 5 pounds." There was a small silence, then his voice, so gentle. "Gloria, that's 10 percent of his body weight. It could be diabetes."

We were given instructions to collect Brennan's first urine in the morning to see if it contained sugar by using special test strips. We rushed to the pharmacy to buy them. The strips turned dark blue, indicating a high concentration of sugar. We called the doctor again and were told to get on the next plane home. We began to pack. We knew it was important that we get Brennan to the doctor, but did not know anything about diabetes, so we didn't understand the urgency of getting him into a hospital. The campsite nurse stopped in. I remarked to her that it seemed a shame to be leaving this special family event when we had just arrived and were going to be home in two days anyway. Did she think we could wait till then? She said, "Probably."

"Could anything happen if we do wait?"

"He could go into a coma." She said it so matter-of-factly, as if a coma were not that much of a problem!

We called and made arrangements to go home. Back in Los Angeles, we admitted Brennan to Children's Hospital. I tried to be in control of all this newness entering our lives. I had always been a great one for control. Everything needed to be in its proper place in the house or I would feel anxiety creeping up on me. I had worked hard to be the perfect wife by jumping to serve my husband's every need. I had held back anger and buried resentment rather than risk confrontation. I had tried to be the perfect mother, breast-feeding Brennan for well over a year, making all his baby food from scratch. I was so proud of his almost perfect health. From the time of his birth at over 9 pounds, he was bigger than most babies his age. Until a short bout with chicken pox, he had never been sick, never even had a cold. He was my perfect child.

For the first days, Alan and I took turns staying at the hospital so that Brennan was never alone. When I wasn't at the hospital, I was home with our other son, Robin. I was very busy taking care of everyone and everything, but was giving myself no time to become aware of what I was feeling. Those feelings could not be put off for long.

They came at 2:00 A.M. on Brennan's third night in the hospital. I gently eased out of his hospital bed and padded down the hall to the pay phone. I dialed home and heard Alan's voice say hello. A scream rose from my belly, filling my mouth, my ears, the air around me. It seemed to go on forever. The sadness was so much greater than anything I had ever allowed myself to feel. I wasn't just crying for Brennan, I was crying for me, too. I had lost my illusions of control.

I had also lost my expectation of an unlimited future for my child. I learned that diabetes is a chronic illness and that insulin is not a cure. I was told that Brennan would take insulin for the rest of his life. I read a statistic which claimed that 50 percent of all juvenile diabetics die within twenty-five years of diagnosis. I was shown a chart of all the possible injection sites: a line drawing of a child with little rows of dots on the arms, legs, buttocks, and stomach where the needles would enter. It was devastating to think of poking my son's little body with so many needles.

At the same time, I learned that diabetes is a disease you can live with, that many diabetics live for forty and fifty years beyond diagnosis. One doctor told me that of all the major diseases, if he had to choose one to have, he would choose diabetes.

We learned how to care for Brennan, to test his urine for sugar, and to give shots. We practiced for two days on oranges. The morning Alan was to give Brennan his first shot, Brennan looked at his father (who had been known to faint at the sight of blood) and said, "Are you any good at this?" When the debut shot was completed, Brennan said, "Pretty good."

PERIOD OF ADJUSTMENT

At the end of the week, we took Brennan home. We'd been to diabetes education classes, but still felt basically unprepared. Brennan had always loved to eat, and now food became an issue. I had always let Brennan eat as much as he wanted of anything as long as it was healthy. I did not keep any sugary foods in the house (which of course made some of the transition easier), but I also didn't allow sodas or Jell-O™ or pudding mixes. I considered them junk food. Now I couldn't let Brennan eat two or three oranges at one sitting or drink apple juice or orange juice to his heart's content. I began to buy diet sodas and sugarless Jell-O and other foods I considered unhealthy. How strange to be feeding those foods to my son in order to assist his health.

Gradually, we got organized concerning food and shots and test equipment and emergency supplies. The list of things to know and learn seemed endless. Harder still was dealing with Brennan's increasing anxiety about the injections. It got to the point where it took two of us to hold him down to give him his shot. So many times "I hate you" was hurled at us. Sometimes, after we'd finally gotten finished, we'd sit and cry together.

Robin was too young to understand what was going on. It wasn't until two years later that he mentioned anything.

"Brennan has diabetes, doesn't he?"

"Yes, honey," I answered.

"What do I have?"

I thought for a moment. "Cute buns."

He seemed satisfied with that answer.

There were many adjustments to be made that first year. We researched the various diabetes organizations and joined two of them. Alan met Lee Ducat, one of the founders of the Juvenile Diabetes Foundation International, and became very excited about the work JDF was doing in support of research to find a cure. I didn't know that anyone in the diabetes field thought a cure was even possible. I made a promise to myself and later to Brennan that someday his shots would be over.

In the meantime, the daily management of Brennan's diabetes became my job. It was not always easy.

A year or so after Brennan's diagnosis, we tried to switch Brennan from urine testing to home blood glucose monitoring. It was a disaster from the first. He was far more terrified of the finger prick than he had ever been of the shots. It sometimes took more than twenty minutes to get a blood test. Those minutes were filled with screaming and rage such as I had never experienced. It left us exhausted. It seemed that whatever good we would have gained from the better blood sugar control we lost through the stress and anger generated by the twice-daily ritual. After about two weeks, we decided we would postpone blood testing until he was a little older.

A CRISIS

It didn't take too long for blood tests to come back into our lives. Alan had taken Robin with him for a weekend trip. I took Brennan and our dog, Marty, along with my girlfriend, Beth, and her daughter, Casey, out to our beach house, where we had a relaxing evening filled with games, TV, and ice cream. The next morning, the king-size bed where Brennan and I were sleeping started shaking. I jumped out of bed convinced it was an earthquake.

It was Brennan. His eyes were rolled back in his head. His body was jerking like a jackhammer. Blood was trickling down from the corner of his mouth. Brennan was having a seizure! I remembered something about people swallowing their tongues and thought perhaps Brennan had bitten through his. I tried to pry his mouth open and realized his jaws were slammed shut. Sugar! He needed sugar. He was having a convulsion because of low blood sugar. I ran upstairs yelling to my girlfriend to wake up and see to Brennan. I had no liquid glucose at the beach house and knew I couldn't get him to swallow regular sugar. Then I remembered that I had glucagon in the refrigerator. When we left the hospital, they gave us the glucagon to be injected if Brennan should ever lose consciousness. I checked the expiration date. It had passed three months ago. It was all I had. I decided to use it and frantically mixed the two bottles into the syringe while calling the doctor. Finally, with her help, I was able to calm down enough to inject Brennan with the glucagon.

Within minutes the jerking subsided. I sat with him, calling him back to consciousness. "Brennan, Mommy's here. Come back to me. Beth's here. Casey's here. Come talk to us, honey." He opened his eyes and asked where his dog was.

We spent the rest of the day trying to keep his blood sugar from bottoming out again. The glucagon had upset his stomach and he kept throwing up. Beth went out and bought blood testing equipment. The doctor had told me that if I couldn't get accurate blood sugar readings, Brennan would have to go to the hospital to be monitored. Brennan was somewhat dazed from the whole experience, so we moved quickly. We used an ice cube to numb his finger and, by using the dog as a distraction, got a finger prick accomplished without war breaking out. We praised him lavishly for being so brave and from then on had no major problems with blood tests. The wall of his fear had been scaled. We used Popsicles™, juice, and chicken soup to restore his blood sugar, although it took about seven hours for the nausea to subside.

It was the most frightening thing that has ever happened to me. I thought he would die if I didn't get the glucagon into him fast enough. Of course, that was not the case, and everything turned out all right. Even the blood coming from his mouth was not as bad as I had thought. He had not bitten his tongue. When his jaw had clamped shut, it had jarred two loose teeth.

One good thing came of it all. I mentioned to the president of the local JDF chapter that I had been completely unprepared for what I saw and went through that day and they arranged to have a special meeting to teach parents how to handle convulsions.

HOW THIS BOOK WILL HELP YOU

Since then, we have never had another convulsion or hospitalization. I have gotten through these years with the help and support of so many wonderful people. I've written this book to help you as I have been helped, and to respond to the many letters from parents who wrote of being overwhelmed by the task of caring for their newly diagnosed children.

Chapter 2, "Everything's Upside Down," is a primer on diabetes and how it affects your child's body. It discusses how insulin works, the tools you'll use to control your child's blood sugar, and the many physical obstacles you'll encounter in trying to achieve good control.

Chapter 3, "Needles, Insulin, Tests, Oh My!," presents all of the practical elements of life with diabetes: your child's doctors and other professionals; blood testing equipment and how-to tips; information about insulin, injections, and attendant gadgets; how to use insulin, food, and exercise to overcome the obstacles to good control; and a list of essential supplies to have at home and at school.

Chapter 4, "Mom, I'm Hungry!," presents the food aspect of treatment, encouraging you and your family to eat foods within the general guidelines of a diabetes diet (foods low in fat, salt, and sugar) and provides tips on how to accomplish that. There is information on the Exchange Diet, the Glycemic Index, and tips for supporting your child's diet plan while eating away from home or on special occasions.

Chapter 5, "Lousy Ketchup," offers your child's view of his diabetes, the ways his view affects his emotions, and how you can help him make the necessary emotional and psychological adjustments. It also offers an overview of some techniques of good parenting you can use.

Chapter 6, "What About Me?," is for you, the parent. It is my way of having an empathetic conversation with you concerning all you're feeling and all you must do. I offer some suggestions to help you deal with the stress of your child's diabetes, give you tips for developing a solid support system around you, and encourage you to become an advocate for your child, asking for and getting what is best for your child at school and elsewhere.

Chapter 7, "Research Moves Toward a Cure," details the history of diabetes research and its present state. Hopefully, it will inspire you to join me in actively raising money to find a cure.

The "Resources" section is a list of the many sources of information and support you have available to you.

2

Everything's Upside Down

None of us will ever forget the day we were told our child has diabetes. So many feelings flooded our hearts, but there was little time to fully acknowledge our emotions. There was too much to do, too much to learn.

As a parent of a newly diagnosed diabetic child, you must immediately assimilate an abundance of new information. You begin to care for your child in new ways. You learn to give shots and take blood tests. You learn what your child should and shouldn't eat. You learn a new vocabulary. You listen and absorb as much as you can. You take your child home feeling barely competent, afraid that some decision you make will endanger your child's health.

I remember the day after Brennan came home from the hospital; he was hungry and asked, "What can I eat?" My answer was "I don't know!" According to his diet plan, he'd already eaten all he should have until dinner. Frantically, I paged through the Exchange Diet booklet to see what I could give him that had no calories. I was a wreck.

Since then, I've come a long way in understanding what diabetes is and how it affects my son's body. This chapter describes how diabetes physically affects your child during everyday living as well as during illness. By understanding exactly what diabetes is doing to your child's metabolism and physical functioning, you'll be better able to use the tools for good blood sugar control that I discuss in chapter 3.

You might want to get a copy of the video version of this book. It is organized in a way that will help you in the earliest days after diagnosis, when you first come home from the hospital, and in looking ahead to what may be. There are many children and parents who share their stories on the video. It will feel like you've gathered a whole support team around you. Ordering instructions are on page 195.

WHAT IS DIABETES?

Diabetes is a complex disease that results in too much sugar in the blood. Your child has juvenile, or insulin-dependent, diabetes, which is technically known as Type 1 diabetes. In people with Type 1 diabetes, the pancreas no longer produces insulin, a hormone essential for life. A person with this type of diabetes needs insulin injections to stay alive. In Type 2 diabetes, also called maturity onset or non-insulin dependent diabetes, the pancreas is still producing insulin, but the body is unable to use it efficiently. This type of diabetes is most often brought under control through a combination of diet, exercise, oral medication, and, in some cases, insulin injections.

Type 1 diabetes occurs when the beta cells in the pancreas that produce insulin are destroyed. The pancreas is one of the organs in the endocrine system that manufactures hormones that control essential functions in the body. In the pancreas, the beta cells produce insulin. Insulin is needed by your child's body every minute to balance blood sugar levels and make it possible for the body to utilize the food it is given.

All the food we eat is broken down into simple sugars, known as glucose, which then circulate through the bloodstream. In order for the sugar to enter and feed the cells, insulin must be present. Think of insulin as the key that unlocks the door to each cell so that glucose can enter. If there is not enough insulin, the cells are not fed, and glucose builds up in the blood. The kidneys are overwhelmed by the excess glucose and expel it in the urine. As this excess sugar leaves the body, it takes a proportional amount of water with it.

Remember the changes I noticed in Brennan—the urination, the thirst, and the weight loss? His pancreas had stopped producing insulin and sugar was building up in his bloodstream. His excessive urination was the result of his kidneys expelling this excess sugar. The kidneys operate under the guidance of a renal threshold, which determines how much sugar they can handle before they excrete it into the urine. This renal threshold differs for each person.

Brennan's increased thirst was his body's attempt to ward off dehydration. He was wetting the bed because his bladder couldn't keep up with the flood of liquid that needed to leave his body. Because there wasn't enough insulin, the food he ate couldn't enter his cells. His body was hungry and it was beginning to break down stored fats to provide an energy source. This resulted in his losing weight.

The physical changes Brennan experienced are the classic symptoms of uncontrolled diabetes—excessive urination, excessive thirst, and unexplained weight loss.

Normal blood sugar for nondiabetic persons will, most of the time, fall within a range of 80 to 140 mg/dl. (The "mg/dl" stands for milligrams per deciliter of blood.) For a person with diabetes, blood sugar is considered high when it is above 140 mg/dl (caused by there being more glucose than insulin), and low when it is below 80 mg/dl (caused by too much insulin and not enough glucose).

The brain's fuel is glucose. When the blood sugar falls below normal, the brain doesn't receive the fuel it needs to function. The adrenal glands then release adrenaline, which prompts the liver to release stored sugar. The symptoms of low blood sugar are caused first by this adrenaline rush and subsequently by the brain receiving inadequate fuel. These symptoms vary from person to person, but are most often characterized by hunger and tiredness, perspiration and trembling, abrupt changes of mood, confusion, lethargy, and, on rare occasions, unconsciousness and convulsions.

I remember one night arriving home from work after dinner. As I came in the door, I could hear Brennan whining in a familiar way. I found him in his father's office sitting on the couch looking miserable. Alan explained that Brennan had been very cranky and out of sorts for the last hour or so. He had been given his shot and had eaten dinner, so Alan was sure he couldn't have had low blood sugar. Yet, I knew that he was acting exactly as if he were having an insulin reaction. I trusted my instincts and took him to the kitchen for orange juice. In a few minutes, the whining stopped and Brennan was himself again.

Brennan must have been sliding into an insulin reaction as he was being given his shot and dinner. We weren't testing his blood sugar then (only urine tests), and had no way of getting a precise reading of his blood sugar. The insulin took effect and would have brought his blood sugar much lower, but by then he had eaten dinner, which had helped to keep him from a serious insulin reaction. However, his brain was still not receiving ample fuel and his dinner was digesting too slowly to raise his blood sugar up to the normal range. I asked Brennan if he remembered eating dinner. He didn't. I asked him how he had felt. "Mommy, everything was upside down!"

TYPE 1 VERSUS TYPE 2

As a parent of a child with diabetes, there will be occasions when you may want to explain the difference between Type 1 and Type 2 diabetes.

First of all, Type 1 diabetes is the severest form of the disease and affects about 10 percent of all persons with diabetes. It can be diagnosed at any age, but is most commonly diagnosed during childhood, which is why it is also known as juvenile diabetes. The beta cells which produce insulin have, to a greater or lesser degree, been destroyed. It is now understood that the beta cells are destroyed because of a combination of genetic susceptibility and immune system malfunction, triggered in some way by a viral infection. (I discuss the causes of diabetes at length in chapter 7.)

An interesting thing happens to most children after they are diagnosed; they go into what is called the "honeymoon phase." This is an undefined period of time when there seems to be a resurgence of pancreatic function, resulting in increased production of insulin. The need for injected insulin may decrease to only a few units. It is very confusing, because it may seem as if your child "almost" doesn't have diabetes anymore. Unfortunately, that is not the case. This phase can last for weeks or even months, but eventually the "honeymoon" is over, and the need for injected insulin rises.

There is another interesting thing that happens. Dr. Robert Rood, one of my diabetes consultants, told me that for three to five years the pancreas still produces some insulin. After that time the beta cells completely cease production and the patient becomes totally dependent on injected insulin. The blood sugar suddenly becomes more difficult to control and this may cause a child who has done just fine on one shot a day to need a two-shot program.

In Type 2 diabetes, the beta cells are still producing insulin, but either it is not a sufficient amount or the body is not utilizing it efficiently.

Onset is usually after the age of thirty-five, and is most frequently associated with a sedentary lifestyle and obesity. Type 2 diabetics also experience high blood sugar, which can usually be brought under control by a combination of diet, exercise, and oral medications. The medications either prompt the pancreas to produce more insulin or help the body use the insulin more effectively.

Type 1 diabetics must inject insulin because insulin is a hormone that, if taken orally, is broken down by the stomach enzymes.

Type 2 diabetics have beta cells that still produce insulin. The oral medication they take is not a form of insulin. It is a drug of one kind or another that helps the body use the insulin it has or increases its production. Sometimes, if their blood sugar levels are badly out of control, they may need to inject insulin for a while. Then, when their levels improve, they stop the injections. This leads people to think that your child may not always need to take insulin.

HOW DOES INSULIN WORK?

In a person without diabetes, blood sugar control is a perfect example of supply and demand. For instance, a person eats, the food is digested, broken down into glucose, and enters the bloodstream to be carried to the waiting cells. The pancreas is alerted to release exactly the right amount of insulin based on how much was eaten.

When the pancreas no longer produces insulin this elegant system breaks down, meaning that insulin must be injected into the body. The purpose of this injected insulin is to mimic, as closely as possible, the body's natural response to eating. In the healthy nondiabetic person, the body always has a small amount of insulin circulating in the blood, which is known as the basal rate. Then the body adds more, known as the insulin response, in response to any food eaten.

You are injecting insulin into your child's body to replace the insulin he no longer produces. Normally, your child's body matches the insulin level to the food intake. With diabetes, your child tries to match his food intake to a preset amount of insulin. Brennan was right about diabetes— everything is upside down!

As a parent you have to play chemist and balance all the myriad elements that affect your child's blood sugar level. It is not easy and it is not fun. It is difficult and frustrating. The only good thing I can say is that, as time goes by, it does get easier and becomes an accepted part of the daily routine.

A BALANCING ACT

The daily routine of a diabetic child involves injections of insulin and blood tests to keep blood sugar as close as possible to the normal range. This normal range of 80 to 140 mg/dl is where your child will feel and function best, with enough glucose to feed the brain and body, but not too much to cause dysfunction and contribute to complications later in life.

In reality, a diabetic child's blood sugar is usually above or below that standard. It's almost impossible to keep a child's blood sugar within the normal range all the time. The point is to keep your child's blood sugar in reasonably good control most of the time.

Good control mimics the body's natural response to food, blood sugar, and metabolism. The long-acting insulins, NPH, Lente, and Ultralente, act over a long period of time to supply a constant rate of insulin, just as the basal rate does. The short-acting insulins, Humalog and Regular, are usually given to cover meals eaten, in the same way the body supplies insulin.

Insulin is only one of the variables you can adjust to bring the blood sugar levels close to normal. There is also food and exercise. For example, one mother finds that the best approach for her daughter is to adjust her meal plan according to her blood sugar levels. Her child is given a little less to eat if she has a high reading, and more to eat if she is low. This mother has found, by trial and error, that her daughter does not respond well to frequent insulin dose changes.

Brennan, on the other hand, has found that adjusting the insulin dose by small amounts keeps his blood sugar in better control without bringing on low blood sugar reactions.

Another mother has her daughter ride her bike, jump on a small trampoline, or use the "Power Pad" on the Nintendo activity system when her blood sugar is higher than desired. Instead of using compensatory doses of insulin, she uses exercise to bring her blood sugar under control.

A note about exercise: It has been observed that if a child's blood sugar is above 300, exercise can add additional stress to the body and may actually increase the blood sugar instead of reducing it. Each child responds differently, so it is best to discuss using exercise to lower a very high blood sugar with your diabetes professional.

CHALLENGES TO GOOD CONTROL

Insulin, food, and exercise are the three basic tools used to try to keep your child's body functioning properly, even though he has diabetes. Wouldn't it be nice if there were a simple formula to use that would ensure consistently good blood sugar control for your child? Sorry to say, there isn't.

Good control is the result of educated guesswork, and there are many obstacles that can get in the way. In this section we'll look at the obstacles: stress, the Somogyi Effect, the Dawn Phenomenon, illness and hospitalization, and the cycle that leads to ketoacidosis. In the following section, I've also included the story of one parent's struggle to control her child's blood sugar to illustrate much of the information in this chapter. Then, in the next chapter, I'll show you how to use the tools that are available to you to overcome these obstacles.

Stress

Stress, good or bad, can alter blood sugar levels because the pancreas is part of the endocrine system that releases hormones in response to stress. In times of excitement or upset the adrenal glands release adrenaline, which is known to raise blood sugar. One teenage girl remembers feeling her blood sugar rise as a handsome new student entered the class. She had tested her blood only thirty minutes earlier, but out of curiosity, excused herself and again tested her blood sugar. It had soared to over 400!

Conversely, high blood sugar can affect emotions and cause mood swings. Some teens find they get angry more easily when their blood sugar is high. Nobody is exactly sure how blood glucose levels affect mood swings, but it is known that rising blood sugar can lead to fatigue and dull mental functions. That's good incentive to keep blood sugars under control, especially at exam time.

It is impossible to keep our children free from the pressures and stresses of growing up nowadays, but being aware that stress may be the reason your child's blood sugar is out of control can help you choose appropriate techniques to mitigate the stress. Chapter 5 looks at the stresses your child may feel and how you can help him.

The Somogyi Effect

The Somogyi Effect is a pattern of bouncing blood sugar. It is the result of hormones released during an insulin reaction that help counter the low blood sugar. The Somogyi Effect frequently happens at night, because the nighttime dose of insulin is too high and the bedtime snack is not sufficient.

The child suffers an insulin reaction during the middle of the night from too much insulin and not enough glucose in the blood. In response to this insulin reaction, the liver releases stored glucose to raise the blood sugar. This glucose raises the blood sugar level, resulting in a high morning blood sugar. Many times, because of this high morning reading the nighttime dosage is increased, bringing on another cycle of insulin reaction and high morning blood sugar.

The Dawn Phenomenon

The Dawn Phenomenon also results in high morning blood sugar readings. It is the occurrence of an early morning (usually 4:00 to 6:00) rise in blood sugar.

The Dawn Phenomenon results from the release of hormones from the adrenal cortex, which produces cortisone, and the pituitary gland, which produces growth hormone. These two hormones have interrelated functions and affect the body in powerful ways. It is known that blood cortisone levels naturally rise during the night, peaking at about 8:00 A.M. Cortisone is known to cause an increase in glucose released from the liver.

Growth hormone is also released during sleep. It can decrease the amount of sugar taken into the cells, leaving more sugar circulating in the blood. The cumulative effect of these two hormones is thought to be responsible for the Dawn Phenomenon.

Dr. Rood offers a possible explanation rooted in distant times, when humans were hunters and gatherers. The early morning rise of hormone and glucose activity was in preparation for the hunt. Nowadays, the most strenuous hunting we engage in at dawn is for the bathroom or our toothbrush.

What to Do During Illness

One of the most difficult times to keep your child's blood sugar under good control is during illness. If the illness is one you will be treating at home, such as colds, flu, chicken pox, and so on, you need to understand the changes that are affecting your child. If your child will be treated in a hospital because of an emergency or preplanned surgery, there is additional advice that is very important.

At Home   For a diabetic child, illness presents a compromise between eating less, which decreases insulin needs, and sickness and fever, which increase them.

During illness, the body automatically increases its glucagon output. Glucagon is a hormone made by the alpha cells in the pancreas. It has the opposite effect of insulin; it raises blood sugar by causing the liver to release stored glucose. This released glucose means more insulin is needed. Fever also raises the metabolic rate (how fast the body uses glucose) and the need for insulin. Therefore, illness accompanied by fever increases the need for insulin. A sick child who is still able to eat normally may thus need more than his usual amount of insulin.

You might think that a child who cannot eat or keep food in his stomach would require little or no insulin, but that's not the case. NEVER STOP YOUR CHILD'S INSULIN INJECTIONS. Your child's body needs insulin at all times in order to function.

Of course, if your child cannot eat, his insulin needs will change. A child with an illness that severely limits intake of food is in the midst of a conflict. Illness increases the need for insulin, yet at the same time the child is eating less and would normally need less insulin. These conflicting needs frequently balance each other so that the insulin dose is often maintained at the normal level or decreased slightly, even though the child is not able to eat.

If your child has a flu or virus that is causing him to throw up, there are special measures to be taken. Food and liquid should be withheld for the first hour after vomiting; then begin to give your child small sips of sugared soda or chips of sugared Popsicle.

If your child throws up more than once, consider giving an injection of Tigan (an antihistamine that works quickly to sedate the brain's vomiting reflex). Ask your doctor about keeping this medication handy at all times, if not in the injectable form, then at least as suppositories. They don't work quite as quickly as an injection, but they're safe and effective.

Whether or not you have Tigan at home, you should definitely call the doctor after your child throws up a second time. In the absence of sufficient liquids, your child's body is more likely to develop ketoacidosis, described in detail later in this chapter. If your child becomes dehydrated but does not develop ketoacidosis, your doctor can put your child on an I.V. in her office to replace lost fluids. This can be much less traumatic than entering the hospital. If your child has ketoacidosis, he must go to the hospital.

During illness, you must monitor your child very carefully and maintain close contact with the doctor. You'll need to test blood sugar more frequently, perhaps every hour or two. A moderately ill child can become seriously ill in a few hours, so it's a time for constant watchfulness.

Urine testing also becomes important during illness. You'll be checking to see if there are any ketones in the urine. Ketones are an indicator of how much fat and muscle is being burned by your child's body. Use Keto-Stix or Chemstrip K to determine if the ketone buildup is "small, medium, or large."

Your doctor may also ask you to keep track of urine volume. If the other test indicators are rising and urine volume is up, your child is getting into trouble. Blood sugar over 400 and large ketones are a red flag indicating ketoacidosis and you should call the doctor immediately. If she cannot be reached, take your child to the hospital right away.

Have someone call ahead and notify the emergency room that you're arriving with a diabetic child. Be sure to ask if the doctor on duty knows how to treat diabetes and ketoacidosis. I know of one instance where a child with ketoacidosis was put on a glucose I.V. Of course, having more sugar pumped into the body heightened the problem and the child almost slipped into a coma.

Normally, your child won't be drinking sugared drinks, but a sick diabetic child who can't or won't eat solid foods needs liquids that contain carbohydrates. It is recommended that a child ingest 30 to 50 grams of carbohydrates every four hours during illness. Twelve ounces of sugared soft drink, apple juice, or herb tea sweetened with 3 tablespoons of sugar would provide 30 grams. This would probably be sufficient for a small child. A child over ten years old would need closer to 50 grams. Popsicles are also good. One father I know poured Coke into an ice tray and then broke it into chips for his daughter.

This information is offered as an approximate guideline. Your child's doctor will provide precise recommendations based on the total picture of blood sugar, insulin and food intake, and other data at the time of illness.

At the Hospital—Emergencies and Surgery   Whether your child breaks a bone, needs stitches, or requires surgery, it is vitally important that all hospital personnel know that your child has diabetes. Emergencies and possible accompanying surgery are the reasons your child should wear a Medic Alert bracelet or necklace at all times (discussed in the next chapter). If your child were in an accident and taken to the hospital for treatment without the hospital staff being informed of his diabetes, the emergency care would not be tailored for a diabetic's needs and might actually be harmful. The Resources section tells you how to order a bracelet or necklace for your child.

If your child has a preplanned surgery, there are a few questions to answer before your child enters the hospital.

1. Is the surgery really necessary? Have you gotten a second opinion and weighed the risks of your child not having the procedure? Does your diabetes specialist approve of your child having this particular surgery?

2. Is the surgeon familiar with diabetes? If not, make certain there is a doctor in attendance who is.

3. What tests and procedures will be done? Have a plan outlined by your diabetes specialist for the control of your child's blood sugar including blood tests, insulin injections, and intravenous feeding (glucose I.V.). Be certain that the surgeon and all attending nurses are well aware of this plan. If possible, have your child's diabetes doctor involved in your child's care during the hospital stay.

It is very important that you take an active role in every aspect of your child's hospitalization. Tell everyone who attends to your child that he has diabetes. Bring your own blood testing equipment, insulin, and injection supplies. Request beforehand to be a part of the team involved in the monitoring of your child's blood sugar. Don't take no for an answer.

Be with your child as much as possible. Don't assume that everyone knows how to care for a diabetic child. Get information beforehand about exactly what medications will be given to your child and clear them with your diabetes specialist. Ask questions about every medication given to your child to be sure it is one that has been approved. Hospital staff occasionally make errors.

The stress of surgery puts an additional burden on your child's body and can send his blood sugar way out of control. Someone who understands this and who can demand appropriate care must be there to speak up for your child. That person is you.

Don't be afraid of being in the way. If you treat the staff with respect and kindness, while standing firm about your child's needs, they will respect you. Besides, many hospitals are understaffed, and most nurses are grateful for the extra help.

At the Hospital—Diabetic Coma   Badly out-of-control blood sugar can lead to ketoacidosis and diabetic coma. It is not necessary to be unconscious for a person to be in a diabetic coma. The symptoms include excessive urination and thirst, large amounts of sugar in the blood and large amounts of ketones in the urine, loss of appetite, nausea or vomiting, weakness, rapid breathing, and abdominal pains. A fruity odor on the breath, a dry tongue, and a semistuporous state are also indications of trouble. If your child is brought to the hospital in a state of ketoacidosis and/or diabetic coma, there are a number of problems to be solved.

The first problem is hydration. Your child will have lost a lot of body fluid, which must be replaced. He should be immediately placed on an intravenous saline solution (not a glucose I.V.!) to rehydrate him.

Your child's electrolyte balance will also need to be corrected. Electrolytes are chemical substances, such as potassium, whose levels may fall dangerously due to the stress of ketoacidosis and subsequent treatment. They must be carefully monitored and restored to normal levels.

Acidosis is caused by too much sugar and not enough insulin in the bloodstream. Your child will be put on an insulin I.V. or given injections every one to two hours. The insulin dosage will be based on blood test readings. When the blood sugar readings fall to between 200 to 300, glucose will be added to the I.V. to prevent insulin reactions. When your child is once again able to eat normally and has stabilized, the I.V. will be removed.

If your child is unconscious, a tube may be placed into the stomach to help drain its contents. During ketoacidosis, all the organs slow down their functions, including the stomach. The danger here is that your child might vomit and aspirate the vomit (pull it into the lungs), and the tube will prevent this.

Blood may also need to be taken from an artery in the arm because the measurements of the severity of the acidosis are best done from arterial blood, rather than the blood from the fingertip used for blood tests. These tests are necessary during the first twelve hours, perhaps longer, depending on your child's improvement.

Ketoacidosis and diabetic coma are states that usually come on slowly and are very frightening to a parent as well as the child. Sometimes they happen in spite of your doing everything you know to do. Let's look at how ketoacidosis gets started and progresses so that you better understand the cause of this emergency.

Ketoacidosis   Ketoacidosis is a state in which the body is being slowly poisoned. It's the state that Brennan was in before he was diagnosed. It begins with too little insulin and too much sugar in the blood.

If there's not enough insulin, the blood sugar rises. The kidneys then expel the excess sugar in the urine. As more and more sugar leaves the body, it takes more and more of the body's fluids with it, causing dehydration. At the same time, the cells signal the brain that they're not being fed because without insulin, the glucose can't enter the cells. The brain then tells the liver to release stored glucose to feed the cells, which adds more sugar to the blood (which can't get into the cells either because of insufficient insulin).

The body's primary fuel is glucose; its secondary source is fat. When fat is burned energy is released, but then so are acids (ketones), which are toxic. When glucose isn't feeding the cells, the body begins to break down stored fats in an attempt to feed itself, but releases poisons in the process.

As the body burns these fats, the ketones make the blood more acidic; hence the name ketoacidosis. As the acidity of the blood increases, it throws off the body's chemical balance. The body tries to compensate for this chemical imbalance with deep breathing, and then more rapid respiration. A child in a state of ketoacidosis may appear out of breath. If untreated, this poisoning progresses to abdominal cramps, vomiting, and severe dehydration. Ketoacidosis cannot be treated at home; it must be treated by medical professionals.

3

Needles, Insulin, Tests, Oh My!

Your child has been diagnosed with diabetes. You've been through a crash course in diabetes management. Now you're loaded down with diabetes paraphernalia that makes you nervous and endless questions that make you even more nervous. This chapter offers a life preserver to help you keep your head above water until you've assimilated all you need to know.

Here you'll find information about all the practical aspects of your child's care: the diabetes specialists and what to expect of them, blood and urine testing, the equipment you'll be using, and the kinds of insulin and how to use them to control blood sugar. There's also information about syringes and insulin delivery systems, and tips for giving injections. We'll look at what constitutes good control and the techniques you can use to overcome the many obstacles to controlling blood sugar, some of which were discussed in the last chapter. Last, there's a list of supplies you'll need if you're just getting started.

YOUR CHILD'S DIABETES TEAM

Ideally, your child should be under the guidance of a team of profession-als who are specially trained to care for children with diabetes. That team should include a doctor specializing in diabetes, a diabetes nurse-educator, a dietitian, and an ophthalmologist or optometrist who cares for diabetic patients.

The Doctor

Your child should be under the care of a doctor specializing in diabetes. If possible, find a pediatric diabetologist or endocrinologist in your area. The best way to locate a good doctor is through personal recommendations from others who are knowledgeable about diabetes. If your child's pedia-trician cannot make a recommendation, call your local JDF chapter or the American Diabetes Association for suggestions. You can also call your county Medical Society for a list of specialists in your area or go to your public library and check the *Directory of Medical Specialists.* It details a doctor's training, as well as what hospitals he or she has worked in, and any specialized experience.

Parents I interviewed told me of the many difficulties they encountered in finding a suitable doctor, especially diabetes specialists who would treat children under the age of five. One family got lucky after years of look-ing for the right doctor and found a pediatrician who has diabetes and takes a special interest in their child. One mother found it very difficult finding a local doctor during a period when the family was on welfare. She had to make a trip to a neighboring community.

Another mother told me of a diabetes specialist who demanded she take her daughter to a pediatrician for normal childhood ailments, yet the pedi-atrician didn't want to treat her because she had diabetes.

Sometimes you must become very creative in finding a doctor. A support group can be a good source of feedback about local doctors and diabetes experts. If you can't find a specialist close to home, check with a teaching or university hospital in a nearby large city. Use a local diabetes nurse-educator and pediatrician/family doctor in combination with a specialist in that neighboring city. The local physician or nurse-educator could provide the advice and support needed for daily care, and you could make the longer trip to the specialist for diabetes check-ups. That specialist would also be available for consultation in case of illness and emergencies.

Be sure that your doctor (or diabetes-specialist colleague) is available by phone on a twenty-four hour basis. This is especially important if your child is newly diagnosed. Don't feel guilty about calling with problems. Diabetes is a disease that requires daily, even hourly care, and your doctor's input is vital to your child's health. As time goes on, you'll find that you and your child will learn to make necessary adjustments without having to call the doctor. When Brennan first came home from the hospital, it felt as if I called our doctor at least once a day asking how to adjust his insulin or food plan based on blood sugar tests. Now we make those adjustments easily and with confidence.

One last note: Keep a list of questions that come up about the specifics of your child's care and the broader aspects of diabetes to take to your child's check-up. We've all walked out of the doctor's office and realized we forgot to ask about "such and such"; take all your queries with you in a written form.

Educators and Dietitians

In addition to the primary physician, you'll want to be in touch with a diabetes nurse-educator and a dietitian. The good news is that these two functions can sometimes be found in one person.

A dietitian has been through four years of college with specialized study in nutrition and science, followed by supervised work experience. To become a Registered Dietitian (R.D.) requires passing a national credentialing exam. In addition, dietitians may go on to earn a Master of Science (M.S.) or Master of Arts (M.A.) degree. Some states require an additional license, possibly adding the letters L.D. (Licensed Dietitian).

A Certified Diabetes Educator specializes in diabetes management and displays a C.D.E. after her name. So, for example, you could find an educator/dietitian who lists herself as Susan Jones, M.S., R.D., L.D., C.D.E. (I get tired just typing it). Whether you have one or two people who fulfill these roles is not important. The point is you need a dietitian who will help you design a personalized diet plan fitted to your child's needs and a nurse-educator who will explain the latest equipment and techniques for good control.

A doctor specializing in diabetes usually has assembled a team that includes a dietitian and a nurse-educator. If your doctor doesn't have such a team or any recommendations, contact the local ADA chapter or local hospital. You can also contact the American Dietetic Association and the American Association of Diabetes Educators for recommendations in your area. Addresses and phone numbers are listed in the Resources section.

The Eye Specialist

When Brennan was first diagnosed, I was told to take him to a pediatric opthalmologist for a once-a-year eye exam. This advice is often given to parents living near a university medical center or large city. If a pediatric opthalmologist cannot be located, an opthalmologist trained in diabetes is also recommended. In some smaller cities where an opthalmologist is not available, you may be able to find an optometrist, identified by an O.D. after her name, who is familiar with diabetes. Whichever doctor you use, your child must have a dilated eye exam, so that the doctor can look at the back of the eye for any changes in the retina.

Dr. Robert Rood notes that eye changes do not usually appear until at least eight to nine years after onset. The American Diabetes Association suggests the first eye exam be scheduled five years after onset. At that time, it might be advisable to travel to a larger medical facility to consult a pediatric opthalmologist every year or so in addition to a local doctor to ensure the best care.

There's a new piece of equipment which can be of value to patients with diabetes. It's a fundus camera, which takes a picture of the retina. These pictures, along with a letter detailing the results of the eye exam, can be sent to your child's diabetes doctor. She will then be able to see exactly what's happening in your child's eyes, can confirm any physical changes that might indicate the early stages of retinopathy, and can also judge the completeness of the exam.

THE EXAMINATION

Your child should have an examination every three to four months, which will include a complete physical examination, a discussion of the blood test records (which should be brought to each visit), and several times a year, a blood test called a glycosylated hemoglobin, or hemoglobin AlC.

The physical exam will include a urine test to check for ketones and factors that are early indicators of kidney problems. It will also possibly include a blood test to check immediate blood sugar. The doctor may need to take blood from your child's arm for the hemoglobin AlC. Your child's height and weight will be measured and compared with "norms" for similar age groups. Diabetes can sometimes delay the onset of puberty and slow a child's growth if it is in poor control, so your doctor will make note of your child's sexual maturation stage. You can expect blood pressure and pulse readings as well as careful observation of the skin, feet, and injection sites.

Many doctors are now doing a routine cholesterol-level check on children. Diabetes increases a person's risk of heart disease and stroke. High cholesterol further increases that risk. A recent study of 6,500 children in Ohio showed that twice as many children had cholesterol levels over 185 than had been expected. A cholesterol level of under 175 is considered acceptable in a child. If your doctor doesn't offer to do a cholesterol check, ask to have it done.

Your child should be testing his blood sugar several times a day. If your child is being treated by a doctor who is not a diabetes specialist and diabetics do not account for a large portion of her practice, she may not have stressed the importance of blood testing over urine testing. Be assured that home blood glucose monitoring is the most important advance in the care of diabetes since the discovery of insulin. There is easy-to-use, computerized equipment (more about this later in the chapter) that will help you and your doctor chart the course of your child's daily blood sugar levels. This information helps your doctor fine-tune your child's control.

The other blood test that is important is the hemoglobin AlC. It gives an accurate assessment of how effective your child's blood sugar control has been during the preceding three months by measuring the amount of glucose that clings to the red blood cells. If your child has a high concentration of sugar in his blood on a daily basis, it is reflected by how much glucose has bonded to his red blood cells. This test gives an indication of the overall blood sugar control for the previous three months. As an example, since becoming a teenager Brennan has not been testing his blood sugar as frequently as I would like. His AlC tests, however, have been lower than they've ever been, so it helps me cut back on the nagging.

Dr. Robert Rood recalls a mother whose child always had a 400 or higher blood sugar when she came in for her exam. The mother insisted that it was Dr. Rood's fault. He made her daughter nervous and the stress was raising her blood sugar. Years later, when the AlC became a standard test, Dr. Rood discovered it wasn't his fault after all; the daughter was out of control much of the time, not just during her visits to him.

Ideally, this test should be done every three to four months or at least twice a year. Hemoglobin AlC test numbers and their interpretation can vary from lab to lab. Generally, a reading of 6 or 7 would be considered not so desirable. Your doctor will tell you what your child's results mean and how to make necessary adjustments of the insulin and testing routine to bring higher test results down to lower levels.

TESTING, TESTING

One of the most important practical elements of your child's daily care is blood testing. Home blood glucose monitoring is a fairly recent development in the history of diabetes care. Years ago, the only way to get a blood sugar reading was to go to the doctor's office or a hospital. Insulin dosages were based on urine tests, which give only an approximation of current blood sugar.

When Brennan was first diagnosed, we used urine testing. I recall a story I heard from a parent about her son's first time at a diabetes summer camp. At the time, everyone still did urine testing. A few of the kids were feeling frisky one morning and told their counselor that instead of doing individual tests, they would all pee into a barrel and the counselor could average it out. That's a good analogy for a urine test!

Dr. Rood told me of adolescent patients who would sometimes dilute their urine with tap water to ensure negative tests at the doctor's office. They foolishly used the cold water. A fresh urine sample is normally quite warm, as it has just left the body. Dr. Rood would stick his finger into the cooled sample and remark, "Either this is a mistake, or you died a week ago."

Blood tests are quite a bit more reliable!

Meters

The technology that supports home blood glucose monitoring is wonderfully simple. You place a drop of blood on a strip and place it in the meter. An electrical charge is stimulated by the amount of sugar in the blood and a precise reading of the present level of blood glucose is given. This new technology correlates very closely with laboratory readings.

There are two types of meters, which are categorized as wipe and no-wipe systems. There is a good reason for this: in one type of meter, you wipe the drop of blood off the strip, and with the other, you don't.

How do you choose the right meter? Your choice should be based on two elements. One is the recommendation of your doctor or diabetes educator, and the other is which model is most comfortable for you and your child to use. The most important thing is that meter fit the ability of the person operating it.

No matter where you buy a meter, make sure the seller provides a step-by-step demonstration. Don't buy a meter by mail order or from a place that has only one or two kinds and offers no demonstration. These little machines are very accurate but only when used correctly.

A nonprofit organization named ECRI (Emergency Care Research Institute) tests medical equipment and publishes a report for consumers. At the end of 1988, they tested eight of the blood sugar meters on the market. They rated three, the One Touch, Accu-Chek, and Diascan, as the most reliable and easiest to use. These three meters range in price from $150 to $200.

When Brennan first started blood testing, the strips could be read visually or by the meter. The new sensor technology does not permit visual reading. If your battery runs out or your machine breaks down, you have no other way of knowing your blood sugar. I agree with diabetes educator Kathy Arrowsmith, who suggests you have a second meter. Many meters cost in the range of only $30 to $65.

Also, never throw away an old meter. Medical companies frequently have trade-ins or rebates for used meters. They can be worth $50 on a trade-in. You might even find a used meter at a garage sale for $5 or $10 to use for such a trade-in. But never use someone else's meter to take your child's blood sugar. There is always the concern of blood-borne disease. The drug companies offer these deals because if you're using their meter, you need to buy their strips. Each machine has its own special brand of strip and they make more money in the long run on the test strips than on the meters.

One more word about test strips—be sure to check the expiration date frequently and don't use them beyond that date.

Some meters can be connected to a machine that prints out the blood sugar readings or can be hooked up to a telephone to send readings directly to your doctor. She may ask you to buy the meter that can provide her with this kind of printout or phone hookup. These printouts give a visual picture of the blood sugar patterns.

How To: Blood Tests

Let's go through each step of the blood testing ritual. First comes the finger prick. You need a piece of equipment that will prick your child's finger as quickly and as painlessly as possible. Brennan used to be afraid of the lancet we used to prick his finger. He could see the little needle that was about to poke him and it made him anxious.

Fortunately, there are models now available that completely hide the lancet. They are fast and virtually painless. Usually, you will get one of these as part of a kit when you buy a blood test meter.

Now for the blood test:

1. Have your child wash and dry his hands thoroughly. Holding his hand below his heart, gently milk the hand from the palm to the tip of the finger to be used. Prick the side of the fingertip, not directly in the center or at the top. The pads of the fingertips are very sensitive and should not be used. The sides have fewer nerves and more blood vessels.

2. Let your child's finger relax for a few seconds before trying to squeeze the blood out. When you've been cut or struck, the muscles tighten up to prevent the release of blood. After a few seconds they relax and the blood flows more easily. If your child is feeling sensitive that day, try rubbing a piece of ice over the spot for just a second or two to "freeze" it. We used this trick with Brennan a number of times when he was resistant to having his finger pricked and it made the whole process easier for him. It probably has more psychological than scientific benefit, but if it helps, use it!

3. Milk the finger from the palm up to the tip to get a good-sized single drop of blood. Turn the finger over so that the drop can drip onto the special pad on the test strip. Follow the directions for your meter or read the strip visually. Note the results in your child's records.

You might be concerned that all these finger pokes are going to permanently hurt your child's fingers. That is not the case. I read about an interesting approach to testing in a story in the Sugarfree Center's

Health-O-Gram newsletter. A diabetic concert pianist didn't want to test his blood as often as instructed because he felt it would make his fingers too sore. He was advised by his doctor to use the same exact place over and over on whichever finger he used least in his playing. That way, a kind of callus would develop at the site and it would hurt less. The doctor stressed that this method would cause no harm to that finger or the callused site.

Researchers in both the private and public sectors are working hard to create noninvasive blood testing methods. JDFI has teamed up with NASA for just that purpose. The astronauts have to test their blood while they're in space and they don't enjoy it any more than diabetics do! The next few years should see the unveiling of new technology that will make blood testing much easier.

INSULIN: YOUR CHILD'S BEST FRIEND

Insulin was discovered in 1921 by Dr. Frederick Banting and his medical assistant, Charles Best. Before its discovery people with diabetes did not live very long lives. Insulin changed that. In 1923, Eli Lilly produced the first commercially available insulin. The first sources were from cows and pigs, hence beef and pork insulin. This insulin was used until 1979, when genetic engineering and recombinant DNA technology produced the first synthetic insulin, which is identical to human insulin.

A national study, the Diabetes Control and Complications Trial, was conducted to determine the effect of tight blood sugar control. By tight, I mean using a physiologic approach to using insulin. When you eat, the body releases insulin in response to the amount and type of food you've eaten. It does this every time you eat a meal. Therefore, it makes sense that mimicking the body's system might be a good idea. That means taking a shot with each meal.

The trial was supposed to last ten years, but after only eight years the results were so conclusive, the trial was discontinued. Tight control, meaning three or more shots a day or using an insulin pump, definitely reduced the complications of long-term diabetes.

One defining factor was the hemoglobin A1C blood test. Having the A1C in the low "sevens", a 7.1 or 7.2, offered as much as 60 percent fewer complications than a reading in the "eights." That's a big difference.

Your child should be on an insulin regimen that provides appropriately tight control, which means three or more shots a day. If you have a doctor who is not a diabetes specialist and doesn't recommend that kind of program, seek the advice of a diabetes educator. I know people who are covered under insurance plans or HMOs that do not send them to a diabetes specialist and they are not getting the most knowledgeable care.

There are four basic types of insulin action: rapid, short, intermediate, and long. Each type differs in three ways: Rapid-acting (insulin analog) begins to work within fifteen minutes and lasts for up to five hours. Short-acting (Regular) begins working in thirty minutes and lasts for up to eight hours. Intermediate-acting (NPH and Lente) begins to work in one and a half hours and last for up to fourteen hours. Long-acting (Ultra Lente) begins to work in six hours and lasts for up to thirty-six hours. These are theoretical time frames. In some people different insulins work faster while in others, the reaction time is slower. The chart below indicates the number of hours for an insulin to accomplish each state of its effectiveness.

	STARTS WORKING IN	PEAKS IN	LASTS FOR
Rapid-Acting	15 minutes	½ to 1½ hrs.	up to 5 hrs.
Regular	30 minutes	2 to 5 hrs.	up to 8 hrs.
NPH or Lente	2 hrs.	4 to 14 hrs.	up to 24 hrs.
Ultra Lente	6 hrs.	doesn't	up to 36 hrs.

Look at the graphs below. Figure 1 illustrates how the blood sugar rises after meals and snacks.

FIGURE 1   GLUCOSE RISE AFTER MEALS AND SNACKS

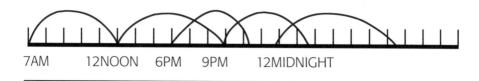

7AM   12NOON   6PM   9PM   12MIDNIGHT

Now look at Figure 2 and you'll see how the two insulins (Regular and NPH), given in two injections, work to cover the rise in blood sugar after meals. The Regular covers breakfast and dinner and the NPH covers lunch and overnight.

FIGURE 2   TWO INJECTIONS

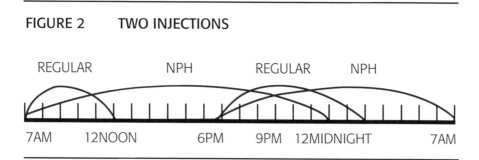

REGULAR   NPH   REGULAR   NPH

7AM   12NOON   6PM   9PM   12MIDNIGHT   7AM

Most diabetic children are on a three-shot program using a combination of rapid-acting, regular, and NPH or Lente. As you can see in the chart, NPH and Lente have similar cycles of effectiveness, and whether your child is on one or the other is strictly a matter of your doctor's preference. Notice the long cycle for Ultralente. It can be a problem because it stays active for over twenty-four hours. Ultra Lente can provide good baseline coverage when the meals are covered with Humalog or Regular. For example, your child could take Humalog or Regular with Ultra Lente in the morning and evening, and only Humalog or Regular at lunch. Ultra Lente is relatively "peakless" and gives a smooth, steady base of insulin, similar to the results achieved with an insulin pump. Ultralente is also formulated with beef insulin, which can cause insulin resistance in some children. Despite these possible drawbacks, I know some children who are on Ultralente and achieving good results.

Until recently, all insulin came from the pancreas of cows and pigs. The most commonly used insulins today are semisynthetic forms of human insulin, known as Humulin and Novolin. They are identical to insulin produced by the human body and are less likely to cause allergic reactions than animal insulins. They are also more readily absorbed.

One anecdotal piece of information: I have heard from many people that when they switched from animal insulin to semisynthetic, they were less able to tell when a low blood sugar reaction was beginning. Of course, these were not newly diagnosed children. They were adults who had had diabetes since childhood. I asked a doctor about this problem and was told there is no proof that the insulin caused this diminshed ability. He said that after years of diabetes, the mechanism that alerts a person to hypoglycemia wears down. Yet each of the people I know experienced this change just after they switched from animal to semisynthetic insulin. Knowing that your child may not be able to tell when he's having low blood sugar can help you and him be more alert for the signs.

The choice of what insulin to use will be made by your child's doctor or diabetes educator. The kind of insulin used may be changed at any time based on your child's condition. (An important note: Only the doctor should change the kind of insulin your child is injecting. Don't let a pharmacist or salesperson tell you another kind will be just as good.)

Don't be afraid to bring information and challenges to your health care professional. For example, Brennan was on pork insulin for many years with no problems, but then he began to develop red welts around his injection site. I reported this to his doctor and we decided that Brennan was having an allergic reaction to the pork insulin at the site of injection. We put him on Humulin and the welts disappeared.

You probably notice that I say "we" instead of just "the doctor." As the parent, I was a part of the decision-making process concerning which insulin Brennan should be using. I had gathered information from other parents whose children had switched from pork to human insulin and presented it to the doctor. He and I discussed the information and he agreed that Brennan should try human insulin. This is an example of how a parent's observation and knowledge can be valuable in assisting and supporting as well as initiating adjustment of treatment.

You are the most knowledgeable person about your child's specific needs because you see him every day. Don't withhold your opinion. Trust your intuition. Share information and ideas both with your child's doctor and other members of your child's diabetes team.

GIVING INJECTIONS

Once your child's blood test is done, you're ready to inject insulin. First, let's talk about what device you'll use to get the insulin into your child's body. The insulin will be loaded into a syringe or insulin delivery system.

Syringes

The syringes sold today are disposable and fitted with very short, fine needles. You'll want to buy the highest gauge needle you can find, which will be a 30- to 31- gauge. The number refers to the width of the needle. The higher the gauge, the finer the needle. The needle length is now ⅓ to ½ inch, which is less frightening to a crying child than the longer ones we used to use.

You can use a disposable syringe more than once. Some parents reuse them to save money and report having no problems. However, Mary Ann Robnett said she hesitates recommending the reuse of syringes because not all families have living conditions that are as clean as they might be. For these families, using a needle more than once could increase the risk of infection. Dr. Rood, on the other hand, reports that many of his patients reuse their syringes.

Discuss the possibility of reusing needles with your doctor or diabetes educator. If you decide to reuse a syringe, be advised that after two injections the needle may become dull. Also, be sure to recap the needle immediately after use, and never use syringes with bent or dirty needles.

Injection Sites

You will be injecting insulin into your child's arm, leg, buttocks, or abdomen. It is important to rotate the injection sites in order to prevent lipohypertrophy, a thickening of the fatty tissue surrounding the injection site that slows the absorption of insulin. Generally, you should not use an injection site more than once every thirty days.

Some kids like to use an injection site more than once because it hurts less, but your child should be informed that insulin promotes fat production and overuse of one site will cause a fatty lump to form. Your doctor or diabetes educator has probably supplied you with a chart on which to keep track of the injection sites. Use it to avoid using a site more than once a month.

Another consideration in choosing an injection site is that insulin absorbs at different rates depending on where it's injected. This provides you another way of fine-tuning your child's control.

For example, if your child's blood sugar is higher than normal and he has to eat soon after his shot, you might want to have the insulin absorbed quickly. Shots in the abdomen are absorbed the quickest, followed by the arms, then the legs, and least quickly, the buttocks. A trick to get insulin to absorb more quickly is to place a warm washcloth over the site before injection, since the warmer the skin, the faster the absorption. Massaging the injection site after the shot also helps speed up absorption. Your doctor and/or diabetes educator will recommend which sites to use.

Exercising an injection site speeds up the absorption and use of insulin. Because of this, it is best not to inject into your child's thighs just before a soccer game or into arms or legs before tennis. The insulin might begin working before the food digests and, combined with the strenuous exercise of a game, could increase the possibility of a reaction.

How To: The Injection

The discomfort of the shot comes from two things: the needle going through the skin (use thin, sharp needles inserted quickly), and the spreading of the tissues by the insulin that's being injected. To avoid pain, inject the insulin slowly. Insulin that is cold can also cause discomfort. We keep the bottles of insulin that Brennan is currently using at room temperature. (Of course, we also have extra bottles in the refrigerator at all times.) The bottles should be used within one month after they are opened. That's not because the insulin goes bad, but rather because of the possibility of contamination from the needle puncturing the top of the bottle so many times.

The atmosphere surrounding "shot time" is important. If you're feeling anxious, take a moment to calm yourself. Take a few deep breaths, think loving, happy thoughts, say a little prayer—whatever helps you relax. Choose a comfortable, peaceful place. Distract your child by talking about the pleasant things that will happen after the shot. Physical distraction is especially good with younger children. Give them something fascinating to play with or examine.

Try not to give a shot in the midst of an argument and don't negotiate with your child over whether or not the shot will be given. It will; there's no choice. Try not to delay. Putting off the difficult does not make it less difficult. Do let your child make what choices he can. Let him choose the injection site or what he'll have for breakfast when the shot is done. Lots of praise and a big hug are the best way to end each injection.

(I remember times when we had to hold Brennan down to give him his shot. I don't think there is anything more heartrending than the cry, "Mommy, don't!" just as you insert the needle. It's easy to give the necessary instructions, but some days it's so hard to follow them.)

There's another interesting perspective to consider. Dr. Rood's adolescent patients say they can tell how their parents feel about them by the way they give their shot!

Before giving the shot, inspect the expiration date and the appearance of the insulin. Do not use it if it has expired. Also, do not use it if the white material remains at the bottom after mixing (leaving clear liquid above); clumps are floating after mixing; or solid particles stick to the bottom or sides of the bottle after mixing, giving a frosted appearance.

Now, let's draw up and inject two kinds of insulin.

1. Gently roll the bottle of long-acting insulin between your hands to mix it; do not shake it. Wipe the top of both bottles with an alcohol swab. (The truth is that we never do this, never have, but this is what is advised by some medical personnel. It's not really necessary if the insulin is kept in a clean place.)

2. Pull the plunger out to the desired number of units of long-acting (NPH, Lente, or Ultralente) insulin to fill the syringe with air. This makes it easier to withdraw the insulin. Holding the bottle upside down, inject air into the center of that bottle of insulin. Withdraw the syringe.

3. Pull the plunger to the desired number of units of Regular insulin. Holding the bottle upside down, inject the air into the center of

that bottle of insulin. Pull the plunger out slowly until you get the number of units needed. Remove any air bubbles by slowly injecting the insulin back into the bottle or by tapping the syringe with your finger. Withdraw the syringe.

4. Insert the syringe back into the long-acting bottle, held upside down, and pull the plunger out to fill with the desired number of units. Be careful not to push the plunger in because it will contaminate the insulin by mixing the Regular into the long-acting. We've done that a few times and have had to discard the contaminated bottle.

5. You may have been told to clean the injection site with an alcohol swab. We never have, except in the hospital when Brennan was first diagnosed. If the injection site is clean, there's really no need. One British study followed two groups of 5,000 people who gave themselves injections; one group used alcohol swabs, one didn't. There were only five infections reported, and those were in the group that used the swabs!

6. Whether or not to inject at an angle is the subject of some discussion. The fatty tissue just under the skin has fewer nerve endings than the muscle which lies just underneath. With a small child, without much fat in his arms, you would want to inject at a 45-degree angle to be certain the insulin enters the fatty tissue layer. For a large child, injecting straight into the buttocks or thighs would probably be fine because there would be enough of a fat layer. It is not dangerous to inject the insulin either way, just more uncomfortable if the insulin goes into muscle rather than fat. Once the needle is in, inject the insulin smoothly and steadily—don't rush. Release the fold of skin and withdraw the needle. Break the needle off the end of the syringe and discard. Discuss the appropriate means of disposing of syringes with your diabetes educator.

Sometimes, parents are advised to pull back on the plunger to see if there's a drop of blood. (This happens if you hit a blood vessel.) It is not necessary and it increases the trauma of the injection process. If you have a child who is squirming or resisting, it is everything you can do just to get the insulin in!

Regarding air bubbles: they are not dangerous when injected into the fatty tissue or the muscle. The reason you are told to get the air bubbles out of the syringe is because they take up the space meant to hold insulin. More air bubbles, less insulin. Contrary to the myth of murder mysteries, your child will not die if you inject an air bubble.

One last word of caution: it's not good to load a syringe too long in advance. Although Regular and NPH can be loaded together long before the shot, the mixture of Regular and Lente should be used within ten minutes after loading the syringe; they interact chemically to form an unstable mixture after ten minutes, which won't stabilize until twenty-four hours later. Rather than try to remember which combination does what, avoid the possibility of a problem by always loading the syringe just before using it.

Gadgets: Insulin Delivery Systems

There are special gadgets now available that offer alternatives to using a syringe. They are called insulin delivery systems. One of them is an innovation from Sweden that assists with insulin delivery. It's called the Insuflon, and is a short, soft, paper-thin tube that is inserted in the abdomen (with a needle that is removed immediately after insertion). This tube remains in place for three to five days, and all injections are given through its resealable opening. This means only one puncture during that time rather than two or three a day.

Mary Ann Robnett advises parents that a device such as this is probably better suited to adults or older teens. Children get much dirtier than adults, which means an increased risk of infection. Still, I feel it's valuable for you to know about all the devices available.

Insulin delivery systems inject insulin into your child in an "automatic" fashion. They can be very helpful.

Infuser Method   In this method, a hollow needle is partially inserted under the skin and taped in place. It can be left in place for several days at a time. All injections are given through this reusable opening. A device such as this is better suited to adults and older teens.

Insulin Pens   These devices are about the size of a fountain pen and load insulin from a cartridge. They can load in ½-or one-or two-unit increments. The advantage of an insulin pen is that it's a very discreet way to take insulin. A teenager might like this kind of system because of its novelty, and because if he's out with friends, he won't have to load his insulin from bottles.

The disadvantage with these systems is that they can hold only one kind of insulin at a time. Of course, that may be fine if your teen is taking only rapid or short-acting insulin at lunch or dinner. Your teen could also use this system if he is using a premixed insulin of 70 percent NPH and 30 percent Regular. Your doctor and diabetes educator can advise you about using premixed insulin.

Automatic Injectors   Automatic injectors take a syringe already loaded with insulin and shoot it into the site quickly. All you do is press a button or plunger. You can use it with one hand, your child can't see the needle (which helps some children's anxiety level), and it gives you perfect injection technique every time. We used one for a while and found it very helpful. Most of these injectors will take any brand or size syringe. Again, don't buy any unit without a thorough demonstration.

Jet Injectors   Another type of insulin delivery system is the jet injector, which uses high pressure to force the insulin through the skin in a jet-propelled stream. It feels like someone snapping a finger against your skin. It does away with needles and you can load two kinds of insulin at once. This kind of jet injection also increases the absorption rate, getting the insulin working faster.

The downside, according to Mary Ann Robnett, is that injectors can cause tissue damage at the injection site. The American Diabetes Association is not recommending that they be used by children until there is more information.

Injectors can be expensive, but of course you'll save a lot of money by not having to buy syringes. Some insurance companies cover the cost of jet injectors when they are prescribed by a doctor.

The Pump   One last system to consider is the insulin infusion pump, which delivers insulin from the reservoir in the pump through a flexible, slender tube into a tiny tube or needle inserted under the skin, usually in the abdomen. The needle and infusion site are changed every one to three days. The pump is compact and sturdy, weighs about three ounces, and is worn around the waist or strapped to a leg or wherever it is comfortable.

The pump is programmed to suit your child's individual metabolism by releasing a continuous trickle of insulin. When it's time for a meal, a button is pressed to release Regular insulin to cover the insulin needs created by that meal. The insulin needs are figured on the basis of blood tests and carbohydrates to be ingested.

The pump is a sophisticated and disciplined approach to diabetes control and necessitates close contact with a diabetes specialist while insulin levels are being determined. There are some children who use the pump, although it is not easy to constantly be "wearing their diabetes on their belt." You and your child can discuss the insulin pump as an alternative with your doctor.

GOOD CONTROL

Achieving good blood sugar control is a daily, hourly battle. The basic weapons at your disposal are the blood test, insulin, food, and exercise. Using blood test readings to adjust your child's food and insulin intake is a skill learned through observation and experience.

I want to say a few words about your child taking more or less insulin. There is no such thing as better or worse when it comes to insulin dosage. There is no right or wrong concerning how much insulin your child takes.

There are three things that matter:

1. Keeping good nutrition habits and eating balanced meals at approximately the same time each day
2. Maintaining ideal body weight
3. Maintaining ideal blood sugar (80–150)

For example, your child has been taking three shots a day for a total of 30 units of insulin. After a pattern of higher-than-normal tests develops you and your doctor decide to add a few units of short- and long-acting insulin to the daily total. Perhaps your child's routine is changed from three to four shots. Don't let anyone tell you that your child is "sicker" with diabetes because he's using more insulin or taking more shots. It's not true. For one thing, it's natural for your child to increase his insulin dose as he matures because insulin dose is based on body weight.

You may want to talk about this with your child. Let him know that he's taking more insulin or one more shot because that's the best way to control his diabetes, not because his diabetes is getting "worse."

Whatever program works for your child is the healthiest and best for him. It's the day-to-day consistency that's important, and that's where balancing insulin, food, and exercise comes in.

Adjusting the Insulin Dose

Understanding the way insulin works is the key to making wise use of blood test information. Of course, in the beginning, it is necessary to call and consult the doctor for changes in the recommended routine. Even during this period your doctor may provide you with a sliding scale showing you how to adjust the insulin dose when blood sugar is higher than desired. As time goes by, you'll assimilate the doctor's approach and feel confident making alterations to accommodate your child's needs.

Blood tests and insulin reactions provide the information by which to adjust the insulin dose. For example, if your child has a pattern of mid-morning low blood sugar and insulin reactions (two to three hours after his shot), his Regular insulin is peaking and he either needs less insulin or more food. If the blood sugar just before lunch is high, he's running out of insulin and the morning Regular insulin may need to be increased.

If the reactions occur six to eight hours after a shot, such as in the middle of the afternoon, then the NPH, or Lente, is peaking and should be reduced.

If your child is suffering reactions in the middle of the night, the evening dose of NPH is the culprit. You'll need to either reduce the dinnertime NPH or increase the bedtime snack. You may find, as some families have, that a third shot of NPH at bedtime (along with eliminating the NPH at dinner) will help put an end to nighttime reactions. That way, the NPH or Lente given at 9:00 P.M. will be peaking between 5 A.M. and 7:00 A.M., instead of in the middle of in the night. The increased insulin activity in the hours before waking allows a child to achieve better early morning control.

It is best not to change the dosage too frequently or too drastically. One or two units can make a big difference, and it's a good idea to wait a day or so on a new dosage to see how your child's body is adjusting. A safe parameter to employ is the 10 percent rule. Look for a pattern of blood sugar readings or reactions, and make the adjustments at approximately 10 percent of the dose of that insulin. For example, if your child is taking 10 units of NPH in the morning and is having high blood sugar before dinner, you would add one unit, or 10 percent of the total of units, and now try 11 units of NPH in the morning.

Of course, you must be very careful when working with small amounts of insulin, since the 10 percent rule might mean giving less than 1 unit. To avoid reactions, you might need to increase the food intake.

The Dawn Phenomenon and Somogyi Effect

Giving a shot of only NPH or Lente at bedtime is also the insulin therapy used for the Dawn Phenomenon. Since the Dawn Phenomenon causes the blood sugar to rise early in the morning, it is best to have the NPH or Lente peaking at the same time.

When dealing with the Somogyi Effect, you need to wake your child and test his blood sugar in the middle of the night to see if it's lower than normal. The 3 A.M. blood sugar tells the tale. If he is having a reaction in the middle of the night that is causing his blood sugar to bounce, you must cut back on the nighttime NPH dose until the nighttime reactions subside.

A note: Dr. Rood cites studies concluding that when a child goes to bed with a high blood sugar (over 200) and wakes up with a high blood sugar, it is not the Somogyi Effect.

The story of one little girl named Lisa is a good example of what happens with the Somogyi Effect. When Lisa was having high morning blood sugar, increasing the nighttime NPH caused even higher morning blood sugar readings. Decreasing the nighttime NPH brought lower morning blood sugars. The more NPH she took, the more severe her reaction, and the more her blood sugar got out of control. The less NPH she took, the less bouncing she did, which meant more consistent, closer-to-normal blood sugars.

High Morning Blood Sugar

The most common cause of high morning blood sugar is inadequate nighttime NPH or long-acting insulin, possibly combined with too much food for the bedtime snack. You and your doctor can try gradually increasing the dose of NPH at dinnertime and/or cutting back on the size of the bedtime snack.

Another cause of elevated morning sugar might be that your child is having low blood sugar in the middle of the night and the morning high sugar is a result of the liver releasing stored sugar in response to the below-normal blood sugar. You can check this by testing his blood in the middle of the night. If the reading is lower than normal, it may mean he had too much NPH at dinnertime or not enough of a snack. This pattern is the way the Somogyi Effect gets started. Once again, discuss it with your doctor and make adjustments.

Another possible reason for high morning blood sugar is that your child may be sneaking extra food around bedtime. All kids help themselves to extra snacks from time to time, especially if they have to follow a restricted diet. You must work that out with your child. For my part, I found crawling under the bed to gather empty Snickers wrappers provided me with the necessary evidence for a frontal assault on the problem!

Treating Reactions

Treating insulin reactions is usually not difficult, although it's easy to go too far and "overfeed." Brennan often feels panicky during reactions and wants to eat everything in sight until the hunger has left, but it takes ten to twenty minutes for a reaction to completely subside. A good guideline is a glass (one-half to one full cup, depending on the size of the child) of juice or some other simple carbohydrate, followed by a small serving of protein and carbohydrate, such as cheese and crackers or half of a peanut butter and jelly sandwich, to stabilize the blood sugar. After fifteen or twenty minutes, test your child's blood sugar and give further food if necessary.

Sometimes the blood sugar falls so low that a child loses consciousness. I was terribly unprepared to handle Brennan's convulsions, as you'll recall. He's only had one convulsion in twelve years, but if it happens to your child, don't be caught as unaware as I was. Have your diabetes specialist take you through a dry run of loading and pretending to inject glucagon so that you will feel competent in an emergency. Always have a supply of liquid glucose and/or glucagon nearby, as well as glucose tablets and cake frosting in a tube. There is a list of supplies at the end of this chapter.

Exercise and Food

Exercise burns glucose, thus making insulin more effective. So, extra exercise means extra food and possibly less insulin. You need to look at the time the insulin will be working at peak efficiency and the time the exercise will take place.

For example, a soccer game at 3:00 in the afternoon will occur just as your child's NPH is peaking. Soccer is a very physically demanding game. In addition to an extra snack, you might consider giving your child a little less NPH in the morning shot. Also, hours of strenuous exercise can result in lower insulin needs for eight to sixteen hours. That might result in a reaction in the evening that is caused by a morning soccer game. Your doctor and nurse-educator can help you plan for these occasions.

Dr. Robert Rood's adolescent athletes are all on four-shot programs of three shots of Regular to cover each meal and one shot of NPH at bedtime. For them, this approach offers the most control and the least reactions.

Postprandial Blood Sugar

If you see that your child has close-to-normal blood sugar before meals, you feel that his control is good, right? Sorry to burst your bubble, but that's not necessarily the case. There's another element to consider—postprandial blood sugar.

Postprandial means "after eating." This reading tells you how well the insulin is covering the carbohydrate in your child's meal. In addition to checking blood sugar before injections, you should also occasionally spot-check the blood sugar two hours after eating, before lunch, and at bedtime to gauge the reading.

The postprandial blood sugar can give a different picture of your child's control than the one you've been getting from before-meal tests. One mother whose daughter's before-meal tests were almost always normal was shocked when the hemoglobin AlC registered high levels. It turned out that her daughter's postprandial sugars were out of control. She was able to bring her daughter's tests under better control by spot-checking after meals and waiting between shots and meals.

Waiting

Letting some time elapse between the shot and the meal gives you another weapon in your battle for good control. This waiting time gives the Regular insulin time to start working before you put more food/glucose into the body. The information listed below is an approximation. You need to tailor the waiting times to your own child based on postprandial blood sugars and your doctor's recommendations. Depending on metabolism and insulin absorption, you may find that your child needs to wait much longer than these recommendations.

With tests of 80 to 150, wait thirty minutes

With tests of 150 to 200, wait forty-five minutes

With tests over 200, wait sixty minutes

I know that sometimes, particularly in the morning on a school day, it's impossible to wait forty-five or sixty minutes. At those times, increasing the insulin will bring higher sugar levels down. Another approach is, if the blood sugar is over 180 and your child can't wait, decrease the amount of food for that meal.

If you're using rapid-acting insulin, Humalog, do not wait. It goes to work very quickly.

Blood Sugar Goals

Toward what level of control should you and your child be aiming? The goal for teenagers is a blood sugar range of 80 to 150 before breakfast or two hours after eating. Younger children should aim for 80 to 180. Preschool children should be kept in a range of 100 to 180. Of course, all these ranges are accompanied by an "if possible."

These are goals toward which to work. Try not to have unrealistic expectations or blame your child if his blood sugar is out of control. Controlling blood sugar is an inexact science. We're trying to artificially reproduce an incredibly complex system. A few higher-than-normal blood sugars are not a disaster. Relax. Work with your child and your diabetes professional to figure out what caused the high tests.

ESSENTIAL SUPPLIES

Now you're ready to stock your diabetes shelf. One of the first things to consider is a Medic Alert bracelet or pendant for your child. Medic Alert is a charitable, nonprofit organization widely endorsed by health groups. It provides twenty-four hour medical information via a toll-free number from anywhere in the world. Your child's medical condition is identified by a personal ID number engraved on the bracelet or pendant. If your child were not in your care and in an accident, Medic Alert could provide lifesaving data to medical personnel attending your child. It's number is 1-800-633-4260.

For Your Home

Below is a list of basic supplies to have on hand at home at all times. Always be sure to check the expiration dates on insulin and blood test strips. In addition, have a second set of all these items in case you run out of something essential at an inconvenient time. (My personal least favorite time is Sunday morning around 8:00. Try finding syringes at that hour!) At home you'll need:

1.   Insulin; two bottles of each kind your child requires
2.   Syringes; they come in boxes of 100
3.   Blood testing equipment
      (a)   Finger-pricking device and lancets
      (b)   Blood test strips
      (c)   Blood test meter
4.   Keto-Stix or Chemstrip K strips for testing ketones in the urine during illness
5.   Insulin reaction supplies
      (a)   Glucagon kit

    (b)   Liquid glucose source: Glutose, Insta-Glucose, Monojel Insulin Reaction Gel, cake frosting in a small tube, or honey in a squeeze-top container

6.   A basket or zip-lock bag filled with:

    (a)   Blood testing supplies

    (b)   Glucose source for reactions

    (c)   Extra food: small cans of juice, boxes of raisins, packages of cheese and crackers. This can be easily transported whenever needed. It's a good idea to keep just such a basket in the car at all times. Some parents keep the above supplies in several rooms of the house so that they are quickly available in case of a severe reaction.

7.   A booklet outlining your child's diet, insulin dosage, and symptoms and treatment of reactions, along with doctors' phone numbers, for the information of anyone caring for your child. (One mother calls her booklet "The Care and Feeding of Bradley." It contains his daily schedule of meals, blood tests, insulin injections, and other useful information.)

8.   A zippered case to hold syringes, insulin, and blood testing equipment that can be taken to a friend's house or a restaurant. We use a man's shaving kit imprinted with Brennan's initials. It houses his daily supplies and can be easily taken with him at a moment's notice.

For School

The supplies you leave with the school will depend on your child's insulin therapy and blood test schedule. You could divide the supplies into two kits as follows:

1.   Shot and test kit containing:

(a) Insulin (if needed during school hours)

(b) Syringes (if needed)

(c) Blood testing equipment (a good idea whether or not your child regularly takes a test before lunch; can be used in emergencies)

(d) Brochures designed for school personnel describing signs of low and high blood sugar and treatment

(e) An index card with your child's allotted food exchanges for snacks and meals with examples and doctors' phone numbers

The list for this kit can also serve as the basis for an earthquake or tornado emergency kit. You would want to add to this list instructions on how to draw up and administer insulin, the dosages and times shots are to be given, and how to visually read a test strip. A special note could emphasize that food must be eaten if insulin is administered.

2. Insulin reaction kit

(a) Quick sugar source: liquid glucose, cake frosting in a tube, cans of orange juice

(b) Snacks to stabilize the blood sugar: prepackaged cheese or peanut butter and crackers

(c) Blood testing equipment

There are important rewards for all the effort to try to control your child's blood sugar. Good control, on an immediate level, helps your child to feel well, have fewer reactions, and stay out of the hospital. In the long run there is every indication that tight control helps your child avoid or delay the onset of complications. That's a goal worth all our effort.

4

"Mom, I'm Hungry!"

Food is an important issue in our lives. It nourishes us on many levels, connecting us to our culture, our families, our emotional and physical selves. It is certainly a central issue in the life of a diabetic child. What to eat, when to eat, and how much to eat are vital parts of your child's on-going health program.

Fortunately for you and your family, the diet recommended for your diabetic child has the same underlying principles as the diets recommended by the American Heart Association and the American Cancer Society. Your child's diabetes gives you the opportunity to reassess your entire family's eating patterns and turn them toward healthier habits.

The information in this chapter will help you support the practical aspects of your child's eating plan. (The feelings your child may have about changes in his diet will be considered in the next section.) I'll discuss how good, basic nutrition affects your child and your family, and show you how to cut back on the "bad guys"—fat, sugar, and salt. You've probably already been introduced to the Exchange Diet, but we'll take another look at it here to reinforce its approach, as well as wrestle with fast foods, artificial sweeteners, and the Glycemic Index. Finally, we'll romp through special occasions—parties, holidays, sporting events, camping, and eating at restaurants and school.

GOOD NUTRITION

Food is one of the tools used to help control your child's blood sugar. Learning all the ways food affects your child takes time, but there are some basic rules which are not too difficult to absorb.

1. Your child's meals and snacks should contain approximately the same amounts of food eaten at approximately the same times each day.

2. Your child should avoid foods that contain a concentrated source of sugar.

3. Your child should follow a diet low in fats and salt to help prevent heart disease and high blood pressure, since he already has increased risk of these diseases due to the diabetes.

In order for your child to stick to this kind of diet, he will need the support of the whole family. This support is going to require some changes in the foods bought and served in your home. The good news is that we are living at a time when it is easier than ever before to incorporate the best principles of nutrition into your family's eating patterns. There is support for healthy eating in most areas of our society, with lower fat, lower salt, and artificially sweetened foods readily available.

There is a vast body of evidence indicating that too much fat, sugar, and salt are unhealthy. Our North American diet of large quantities of fat-intensive animal protein and nutrition-poor treats is seen as a major contributing factor in heart disease, cancer, obesity, and Type 2 diabetes.

My interest in good nutrition began over twenty years ago, long before my son was diagnosed. I followed what was, at that time, considered a "health nut" diet. I never used white flour or white sugar (well, almost never), ate plenty of steamed vegetables and whole grain products, and allowed no red meat to touch my lips. The birth of my two sons brought an expansion of that lifestyle; I breast-fed both of my sons and made all their baby food from scratch. Cookies and sodas were considered special treats. Because of all that emphasis on healthy eating, we did not have many changes to make when Brennan developed diabetes. It's interesting for me to see that the same diet that was once considered extreme is now recognized as essential for optimum health.

The essential elements of a nutritious eating plan are foods that are as close as possible to their natural state. A simple rule is "the less processing, the better." Buy and use fresh foods as much as possible and avoid food products that come in boxes. Choose whole grain products, not grains and breads that have been stripped of much of their fiber and nutrition by degermination and bleaching. Choose fresh or frozen vegetables, fresh fruits (hopefully without pesticide residue). Choose fiber-rich foods, which contribute to the health of the metabolic system as well as slowing down the process of digestion so that the blood sugar rises more gradually.

To cut down on fats, eat fish and chicken instead of red meat. When you do eat red meat, choose lean cuts and prepare them with as little fat as possible. Try to cut down as well on the amount of animal protein your family eats. High-protein diets cause the kidneys to work harder in order to get rid of waste products. Some researchers believe that overworking the kidneys can contribute to diabetic kidney disease, and their research shows that a diet moderate in protein may help prevent or delay kidney disease.

Notice how much animal protein your diabetic child and your family actually eat on an average day. For example, the Recommended Daily Allowance for protein during adolescence is 44 to 56 grams, depending on age and gender. Two glasses of milk and two 3-ounce servings of meat supply 57 grams of protein. Each slice of bread you add is 3 grams of protein. As you can see, it is easy to eat far more protein than we need. There are many ways to help your family eat less animal protein and more complex carbohydrates. Ideas for putting these directives to use are included later in this chapter. I also recommend Jane Brody's *Good Food Book: Living the High-Carbohydrate Way* as a good initial source.

Family support is a vital element in diabetes management. It doesn't mean that no one in the family can ever again eat candy or enjoy a dessert. What is important is that your family eat the same meals as your diabetic child. Besides being good for your family's health, it is a loving way to psychologically support your child. If the low sugar, salt, and fat cooking approach means major changes, do it a little at a time. People like to eat what they're accustomed to and you don't need to create resentment with sudden changes. Let's get into the specifics of how to make those changes.

Fat Facts

In the average American diet, fat (which includes oil) accounts for more than 40 percent of our total calories. Most of the fat is nothing more than empty calories, containing no essential nutrition. One tablespoon of vegetable oil a day would satisfy our nutritional requirement, yet we now consume, on average, the equivalent of ¼ lb. of butter a day, or eight times the necessary amount. Fat also produces 2¼ times more calories than protein: there are 9 calories per gram of fat compared to 4 calories per gram of protein.

Fat and its partner, cholesterol, are culprits in the two most deadly diseases, cancer and heart disease. Fat is a real concern for diabetics since they have an increased risk of heart disease. True, the body manufactures its own cholesterol (serum cholesterol), but it is handled differently from the cholesterol we ingest. Studies indicate that internally manufactured cholesterol results in the formulation of hormones, cell membranes, and protective sheaths for nerve fibers. Dietary cholesterol, however, enters the general circulatory system and takes a direct route to the blood vessels. Cholesterol buildup in blood vessels leads to atherosclerosis, which contributes to strokes and heart disease. Lowering dietary cholesterol is a good idea for everyone.

Saturated Fats   There are two basic categories of fat: saturated and unsaturated. Saturated fat, which increases the amount of cholesterol in the blood vessels, is solid at room temperature. Animal fats as well as two vegetable fats, palm oil and coconut oil, are saturated. They're used in processed foods because they're cheap and don't turn rancid easily. Read labels and avoid products using these two oils, as well as those made with hydrogenated and partially hydrogenated vegetable oil. Its chemical structure has been altered, and it affects the body more like a saturated fat than a vegetable oil. Many peanut butters have partially hydrogenated vegetable oil added, so try to avoid those brands.

Saturated animal fats are not good for your heart as a general rule. However, there is an exception. The fats found in fish are less saturated and, according to recent studies, may be good for you. Fish oil contains a group of substances called Omega-3 long-chain fatty acids. When consumed frequently these appear to be effective in reducing the risk of heart disease. Heart experts are now urging more frequent consumption of fatty fishes such as tuna, sardines, salmon, swordfish, trout, and herring. In addition, squid and shellfish have a high proportion of Omega-3 long-chain fatty acids. Mussels, oysters, scallops, and clams are especially desirable because they are low-cholesterol foods as well. Shrimp is relatively high in cholesterol compared to other fish, but the amount is only one-third of that found in one egg yolk. Shellfish is generally low in fat and low in calories.

A word of caution—because of the long disregard for our environment, we are now being advised to find out where the fish we eat have been caught in order to avoid the toxic wastes that have accumulated in our waterways. To avoid possible toxic chemicals the fish may have ingested, it is recommended that we buy fish from deep ocean waters or farm-raised fish. For example, since catfish are bottom-feeders and are more likely to feed on the chemicals dumped in rivers, only buy farm-raised catfish. Ask the butcher at the market about the source of the fish it sells.

Unsaturated Fats   Unlike most saturated (animal) fats, unsaturated fats are derived from vegetable sources. These vegetable oils, which are liquid at room temperature, don't have adverse effects on blood cholesterol. Both polyunsaturates such as corn, sesame, sunflower, and safflower oil, and monounsaturates such as peanut, avocado, canola, and olive oil, help lower blood cholesterol. Recent studies indicate that monounsaturates have some special properties that may further help our hearts. They are the main fats used in Japan, Greece, and Italy, where heart disease rates are very low, and there seems to be a correlation between their use and those low rates.

All that is needed is 1 tablespoon of vegetable oil per day to supply our requirements of essential fatty acids. It is important not to become obsessive about the use of polyunsaturates since there have been indications that eating too much of them may increase the risk of cancer. In addition to the possible health benefits, I recommend using a monounsaturate such as olive oil for cooking because it can be heated to a rather high temperature before it breaks down and starts smoking.

It is not enough to merely switch from butter and lard to vegetable oils. Health officials are emphasizing the need to decrease the total amount of fats in our diets. The percentage of dietary fat seems to be an important factor in the development of disease. A study of Japanese women found that when they lived in Japan and had a low-fat diet of under 20 percent, there was a very low incidence of breast cancer. After moving to America and changing their dietary fat intake to 25 to 30 percent, the incidence of cancer among these women was raised to our national level of one in ten.

To summarize the issue of fats: It is best to cut down your family's overall intake of fat to under 30 percent (better yet, under 25 percent), avoid animal fat (butter and lard), use vegetable oils sparingly, and when you do use oils, use monounsaturates most frequently.

In order to cut down our fat to under 30 percent, we must know how to compute percentages of fat calories. For example, 8 ounces of low-fat milk has 140 calories and 5 grams of fat. Each gram of fat has 9 calories. So, 5 grams of fat has 45 calories. Approximately one-third (45) of the calories in one cup of low-fat milk (140) are from fat. Extra-light milk (1 percent) has 120 calories and 2 grams of fat. Two times 9 calories equals 18 calories. Hence, only one-sixth (18) of the calories in extra-light milk (120) comes from fat. Milk marked 1 percent has 50 percent fewer fat calories than milk designated as 2 percent.

Until recently I didn't understand the enormous disparity between percentage of fat and percentage of fat calories. Every time you buy a packaged product, look at the grams of fat and multiply by 9. If that number is more than 25 percent of the total calories, try to avoid that product. It takes time to read all the labels and make these choices, but it gets easy as time goes on and is worth it.

Low-Fat Cooking and Eating Tips

1. Use nonstick pans for cooking. They come in a variety of styles from skillets to baking sheets to muffin pans.
2. Use the smallest possible amount of oil or butter for sautéing. Sometimes ½ teaspoon will do when a recipe calls for ¼ cup. Wipe the oil across the pan with a paper towel or pastry brush. Even better, use chicken or beef stock or the liquid from an ingredient you will add later, such as canned tomatoes.

3. Use a steamer rack for vegetables or else cook them loosely covered in a microwave for four to five minutes with a spoonful or two of water. It has the same effect as steaming. By the way, vegetables lose the lease amount of nutrients when cooked in a microwave. (But don't use a microwave to cook vegetables with tight skins such as peas because they will burst as the steam builds up inside.)

4. Trim all visible fat from meat before cooking. Broil or bake instead of frying. Poach chicken or fish in broth or vegetable juice.

5. Remove the skin from the chicken before cooking unless you're roasting it. Sixty-two percent of the calories from unskinned chicken are from fat.

6. Plan ahead when cooking soups or stews that contain fat. Allow them to cool (if possible, refrigerate), and skim off the fat before you reheat and serve.

7. Use homemade chicken, turkey, and beef stock. Save leftover bones in the freezer. When you have enough, put them in a soup pot and cover with water. Simmer for several hours. Add a cut-up onion, a few sliced carrots, and a stalk or two of celery. Strain, refrigerate, and then skim the congealed fat. To get the fat to congeal quickly, stir an ice cube or two into the broth. You can freeze the broth in ice cube trays and pop out a cube or two for sautéing.

8. When you buy meat, choose the leanest cuts. For beef, these are sirloin tip, eye of round, round steak, chuck with round bone, flank steak, tenderloin, lean stew meat, and extra-lean ground beef. For pork, try pork loin or tenderloin, center cut ham, and Canadian bacon. For lamb, use the leg, lamb steak, or sirloin chops. All cuts of veal are lean except the breast.

9. Avoid processed meats such as bologna, salami, sausage, and frankfurters. Leaner choices are sliced turkey breast, turkey ham, roast beef, and any of the new, nearly fat-free versions of ham, chicken, and turkey cold cuts. Watch for nitrates and nitrites that

are used in processing. They are carcinogenic—simply put, they can cause cancer. Check the label and avoid these products if possible.

10. Get rid of bacon. It is high in fat and salt and has added sugar. It adds nothing to your family's health. Bacon and other preserved meats are processed with sodium nitrate and sodium nitrite. If your family is used to bacon or some form of meat in the morning, try sausage processed without nitrates or a plain hamburger patty instead (using extra-lean ground meat). If you must use bacon occasionally, try Canadian bacon or pancetta, an Italian bacon available in Italian delis. Pancetta is cured with salt but without nitrates. Health food stores also carry bacon cured without nitrates.

11. Buy tuna packed in water. You save 200 fat calories per serving.

12. Use low-fat milk (2 percent) at 140 calories per cup, or extra-light (1 percent) at 120 calories, or best yet, skim milk at 86 calories per cup. Use evaporated skim milk for cooking.

13. Buttermilk, in spite of its name, is actually low in fat when made from low-fat milk. Use it to replace milk in pancakes and baked goods (add ½ teaspoon of baking soda to the dry ingredients for each cup of buttermilk).

14. In most recipes calling for sour cream, you can substitute plain nonfat yogurt and save 61 grams of fat and 349 calories per cup. To keep yogurt from separating when cooking or stirring vigorously, first mix 1 tablespoon cornstarch and 1 tablespoon yogurt together, then stir into the yogurt used for cooking. Buy low-fat or nonfat yogurt.

15. Use low-fat cottage cheese, ricotta, and part-skim Mozzarella. Whipped cream cheese has one-third less fat than regular cream cheese, spreads more easily, and you may use less. There are several low-fat cheeses now available. Generally, use cheeses occasionally and sparingly.

16.   Consider using diet margarine. It contains half the fat of regular margarine. Choose the brand which has the least amount of hydrogenated oil. For example, Weight Watcher's® has 1 gram of saturated fat (partially hydrogenated soybean oil) and 3 grams of polyunsaturated fat (liquid soybean oil) versus Fleischmann's Lite which has 2 grams saturated and 3 grams polyunsaturated fat. Whipped butter also contains less fat and calories than regular butter.

17.   Try the new "no-oil" salad dressings or make your own.

18.   Buy "old-fashioned" or "natural" peanut butter that has not had sugar or hydrogenated oils added.

19.   Eat more turkey. It's cheap, nutritious, and lower in fat than chicken.

20.   Eat more whole grains, cereals, beans, pasta, corn, starchy winter vegetables, and rice for complex carbohydrates, fiber, and protein without the fat and cholesterol.

21.   Try to include more fish in your diet. A study of 852 middle-aged men showed that eating fish once a day cut the death rate from heart attacks in half. Also, at Oregon Health Sciences University, twenty patients given a diet rich in fish oils had a 45 percent drop in cholesterol level.

22.   Choose recipes that call for a maximum of a few tablespoons of butter or oil. Do not eat deep-fried foods. Find alternatives such as "oven-fried" chicken.

23.   Stay away from commercial granola and "natural" cereals. They have too much added fat and sugar. The sugar takes many forms— honey, brown sugar, corn syrup, and molasses. The fat is usually saturated animal fat, coconut or palm oil, or hydrogenerated soybean oil.

24.   Investigate foods prepared with Simplesse, a new, all-natural fat substitute. It's made of egg white and milk protein cooked and

blended to resemble the texture of fat. It's being used in a variety of foods from salad dressing to ice cream.

Sugar and Sweeteners: How Sweet It Is

Eliminating sugared foods from your child's diet is one of the tougher aspects of dealing with diabetes. The shots and tests can be done with your child safely under your wing. But, every day, everywhere he goes, there will be sweets to tempt him. Telling your child he shouldn't eat sugared treats isn't enough. You need to set an example.

The best way to start is not to have foods such as candy and sugared jams, syrups, and gelatins in the house. This doesn't mean, as parents, we have to be fanatics. Your diabetic child can certainly enjoy a treat such as ice cream or frozen yogurt when you use it as part of the allowed exchanges or, for special occasions, cover it with extra insulin. Basically, however, sugar intake should be kept to a minimum. While there are artificial sweeteners that allow your child to enjoy a wide range of sweet treats, a good approach to use is that desserts are served infrequently, not as an everyday occurrence.

The difficult part of the sugar issue can be siblings and peer pressure. Depending on the age and attitude of your child, the problems can vary. Completely banning all sweets from the home may cause a family uprising, but there's a good middle ground you can walk and several paths to it.

When your child is first diagnosed, the family may with firm resolve decide voluntarily to ban all sweets from the house. But as the novelty of diabetes wears off, the sweets may start reappearing. If your family has been used to iced cookies, oversweetened Danish and coffee cakes, and a freezer full of Sara Lee, you will all have a tough job. If your family wants to be in better health, in addition to supporting its diabetic member, you'll need to make some changes. Here's some ammunition that may help you institute the changes.

Sugar provides *none* of the forty-four nutrients essential for life. Currently, one-fifth to one-quarter of our daily calories comes from sugars that are added to foods. If you add the two-fifths of our daily calories that we eat as fats, that means we have to get 100 percent of our daily essential nutrients from just 40 percent of the calories we consume. Doesn't sound like a very efficient diet, does it?

As a nation, we consume more than 120 pounds of sugar a year per person. Sugar not only totally lacks nutrients but also uses up vitamins and minerals in the process of being metabolized, meaning we actually lose nutrients by eating it. To make matters worse, most heavily sweetened foods are also high in fat and are a highly concentrated source of calories. A 1-ounce candy bar contains the same amount of sugar (and three times the calories) as a 5-ounce apple but takes up very little space in your stomach. It's easy to overeat when you have a well-developed sweet tooth.

The best thing you can do is wean your whole family from excess sugar. This can be accomplished by doing some home baking and purchasing fewer sweets. Naturally sweetened jams, "lite" or dietetic syrup, and plenty of fresh fruit help. A box of beautiful ripe strawberries can be a special treat, as it is to my boys. You can begin to think of foods that are not sweetened as treats. Bagels, fresh from the bakery, are favorites at our house. It's a task to undertake gradually, but believe it or not, tastes do change, and some foods that your family once gobbled up will now taste too sweet.

You can let siblings have an occasional candy bar, but ask them to be sensitive to your diabetic child's feelings. Brennan sometimes gets upset when Robin eats something he can't, so Robin usually eats the "forbidden" food when Brennan's not around. There are very good dietetic hard candies and chocolates sweetened with sorbitol or mannitol available if you feel the need to keep some on hand.

That brings us to artificial sweeteners. It's not easy having diabetes in our oversweetened country. Thanks to the wonders of modern chemistry, we have ways to sweeten our foods other than using sugar and its cousins—honey, molasses, and corn syrup. However, whether these alternative sweeteners are safe has been questioned.

Saccharin has been shown to cause cancer in test animals when they are fed large amounts of it, but those studies haven't been directly correlated to humans yet. Recently, there have also been questions about aspartame.

As parents, it's hard to know what to do. We don't want to feed our children foods that might be harmful. We need to look at those words "might be." We don't know for certain that our child will be harmed by a diet soda or two each day and a few artificially sweetened treats a week. We do know that a child who feels like an outcast because he can never eat the kinds of foods his friends eat is more likely to sneak undesirable foods. We might not know for certain what artificial sweeteners will do, but we do know for certain what diabetes can do. So we make a trade-off. We trade the uncertainties concerning artificial sweeteners for good blood sugar control and the decreased possibility of complications.

The two most widely used artificial sweeteners are saccharin and aspartame. They are a little different in their makeup and their uses. Saccharin contains a molecule that is not metabolized. It's sold under the names Sugar Twin and Sweet N' Low®. It is used in baking but can leave a bitter aftertaste in large amounts.

Aspartame is marketed as NutraSweet® and Equal®. It is made up of two amino acids that are building blocks of protein. A scientist discovered it when he happened to lick his fingers while conducting an experiment and noticed a very sweet taste. A natural food element, it is metabolized normally by the body. It cannot be used for cooking since it breaks down at the boiling point (212°F) and loses its sweetness. Some people are allergic to it and may experience dizziness and headaches. If that should happen, simply discontinue use.

There are some additional concerns that consuming large amounts on a daily basis may create an imbalance which affects the neurological functions of the brain. The Food and Drug Administration has recommended that ingestion of aspartame be limited to 50 mg per kilogram of body weight. That translates as approximately one 12-ounce can of diet soda per 10 pounds of child. A four-year-old weighing 36 to 40 pounds should limit his intake to four cans of soda a day. That may seem like a lot, but it might be easy to exceed the recommended limit when you include items such as sugar-free pops, gelatin, and drink mix.

An additional reason for limiting soft drinks is that they have a low pH and are quite acidic. Acid works to break down tooth enamel at a high rate and causes tooth decay. It doesn't matter if soft drinks are sugared or sugar free, they're bad for our teeth.

Sorbitol and mannitol are sugar alcohols that metabolize in the same way as other sugars, but are absorbed more slowly. They do, however, raise blood sugar and are not a basically "free" sweetener such as saccharin or aspartame. If eaten in large amounts, they can cause constipation and gas. Discuss these sweeteners with your dietitian.

There is a new sweetener called Ace-K or Acesulfame-K. It is packaged as Sunette® or Sweet One®. It was approved by the FDA in 1988, and has an advantage over NutraSweet in that it keeps its sweetness when cooked at high temperatures. It has essentially no calories, is considered very safe, and has been in use for over five years in Great Britain with no reported problems. It is currently available in fifteen countries.

A quick word about fructose. Fructose is one of the sugars found in fruit. It can sometimes be used successfully as a sweetener by diabetics with excellent blood sugar control (most blood tests between 80–140). With adequate insulin in the body, the fructose will be stored as glycogen in the liver instead of entering the bloodstream as sugar. Several parents I interviewed use fructose for sweetening cookies because they found it did not raise their children's blood sugars very much. Again, check with your dietitian.

The key is moderation. Just as we don't want our other family members to have an overdeveloped sweet tooth, we don't want our diabetic to have an overdeveloped artificial sweet tooth! Diet drinks shouldn't be the only thing your child drinks. (In addition to concerns about aspartame, the phosphates in carbonated drinks interfere with the absorption of calcium.) Desserts can be an occasional treat and your child does not have to give up going to birthday parties or avoid everything sweet for the rest of his life.

Salty, Saltier, Saltiest

Other than sugar, salt is the nation's leading food additive. We consume more than 15 pounds of salt a year per person in this country. Salt is a potential killer for anyone who is sensitive to the blood-pressure–raising effects of sodium. People with diabetes need to be especially cautious of anything that threatens their circulatory system since they are already more likely to develop heart disease.

The biological need is for about 220 milligrams of sodium daily, the equivalent of $\frac{1}{10}$ teaspoon of salt. The recommended salt intake is 1,100 to 3,300 milligrams of sodium for adults or the equivalent of $\frac{1}{2}$ to $1\frac{1}{2}$ teaspoons of salt. We now consume between 2 and 4 teaspoons a day on the average.

The harmful effects of salt on blood pressure were first suggested in 1904. Studies among the Japanese, Eskimos, and Americans have demonstrated a direct relationship between salt consumption and higher blood pressure. Even a study with six-month-old infants showed that they had lower blood pressure when fed a low-sodium diet (breast milk only) than when fed a diet of infant formulas and other foods.

Salt enters our diet in three ways. About one-third is naturally present in the foods we eat. Another third comes from salt added to foods we are served. The final third comes from food processing. For example, one serving of an ordinary canned soup contains 1,000 or 1,500 milligrams of sodium, more than one day's recommended intake. One fast-food meal of a burger, fries, and a shake contains twice the recommended sodium. An ounce of some breakfast cereals contains more sodium than salted peanuts.

Human beings evolved on a diet that was not only low in sodium but also contained ample amounts of potassium. Potassium helps protect against high blood pressure and is found in fresh fruits and vegetables. The more processed foods we eat (high in sodium), the less fresh food we eat. Once again, the nutritional message is clear. Eat foods as close to their natural state as possible. Fresh is best. The next choice should be frozen foods. Use canned goods infrequently. Check the new low-sodium canned foods now available. Read labels. Gradually switch your family to foods with lower sodium.

A preference for salted foods is an acquired taste. Just as you can retrain your taste buds to enjoy foods low in sugar, you can change your taste for salty foods. Introduce less salty foods gradually so that your family has time to adjust. I'm not suggesting you live salt free, just that you will be much healthier with a lower overall intake of sodium. Here are some ways to begin that retraining process without sacrificing good taste!

Tips for Lowering Your Salt Intake

1. If possible, rinse processed foods prepared with salt. Canned green beans and canned tuna are good examples.

2. Read labels. Sodium is also in brine, MSG, soy sauce, baking soda, and sodium citrate.

3. Reduce salty seasonings such as soy sauce, miso, barbecue sauce, garlic or onion salt, dry soup mixes, bouillon cubes, ketchup, and oyster sauce. Use more herbs and spices, garlic and onion (fresh or powdered), fresh ginger, lemon, lime, vinegar, and wine. Worcestershire sauce has much less sodium than soy sauce. There is also a reduced-sodium soy sauce available now by Kikkoman®. (Chun King has 1,479 mg of sodium per tablespoon compared to 930 mg for Kikkoman's soy sauce.) You can also try this trick— by the extra-large–size soy sauce and refill a smaller bottle with one-third water.

4. Try low-sodium baking powder. You might try doubling the amount called for in the recipe. Buy it in health food stores if your supermarket doesn't carry it.

5. Buy unsalted snacks. Crackers, potato chips, pretzels, and corn chips are now available without added salt. Make your own popcorn and sprinkle just a little salt or, better yet, none.

6. Try some of the new sodium-free seasoning or make your own with this American Heart Association mixture:
HERB MIX
½ teaspoon cayenne
1 tablespoon garlic powder
1½ teaspoons each basil and parsley
1¼ teaspoons each thyme and savory
1 teaspoon each onion powder, mace, and black pepper
Put all ingredients in blender jar and blend until they are ground.

7. Remember every ½ teaspoon of salt you add to a recipe adds 1,065 milligrams of sodium to the total. Divide that number by the number of servings and you'll know how much sodium you're adding.

8. Use homemade stocks stored in your refrigerator as needed for soups, sauces, sautéing, and cooking vegetables. Or dilute canned broth with an equal amount of water.

9. Start using some of the "no added salt" and "reduced salt" canned goods and processed foods.

10. Watch for sodium levels in cereals, as they can be very high. Reasonable amounts of sodium, less than 200 mg, can be found in Nutri-Grain®, All-Bran™, Product 19, and Grape Nuts™ brands. Also, many of the cereals found in health food stores are low sodium.

Fiber and Complex Carbohydrates: The Good Guys

Fiber is plant material that cannot be digested by human beings. It is found in unrefined grains (whole wheat, brown rice, corn, millet, barley, and rye), dried beans, peas, fruits, and vegetables. In the past, the food industry removed much of the plant fiber through processing, refining, and precooking, selling us what I call "balloon bread," foods filled mostly with air. Nutritionists and health care professionals now say that fiber is important in the American diet, and we should eat more of it. There are many reasons for this.

On the whole, fibrous foods take longer to eat and, therefore, slow down the rise of blood sugar. Fiber fills you up, taking space in your stomach and intestines, absorbing water and slowing down digestion so you feel full longer. In the large intestine fiber helps eliminate solid wastes and is recommended to reduce the risk of colon cancer. High-fiber food can also lower blood pressure and decrease blood fat levels. This is important to people with diabetes as well as the general population.

There are two types of fiber. One is insoluble, found in whole grains and bran. The types of insoluble fiber are cellulose, hemicellulose, and lignins, and are indigestible. These add bulk, hold water, and help move food through the body, as well as assist in lowering overall blood cholesterol.

Soluble fiber includes guar, pectins, and gums, which are water soluble and are found in fruits, vegetables, beans, legumes, and cheap ice cream. (They are less expensive than cream and help to gel and thicken the ice cream.) They form a gel in the stomach and cause food to be held longer, resulting in a slower rise in blood sugar. Foods rich in starch and fiber such as oats, beans, and whole grain breads seem to increase the body's sensitivity to insulin and can sometimes lower insulin requirements.

In one study reported in the *British Medical Journal,* researchers discovered that the greater the amount of whole, unmilled kernels in the bread, the more slowly the bread digests, and therefore causes glucose levels to rise more slowly and to lower levels. They concluded that "breads containing a high proportion of whole cereal grains may be useful in reducing the postprandial glucose (after meal rise in blood sugar)."

Starchy foods high in fiber are also good sources of nutrients. The potato is a good example. A 5-ounce potato provides about 5 percent of your daily caloric needs, but 6 percent of your protein; 8 percent folacin, phosphorus, and magnesium; 10 percent iron, niacin, and copper; 15 percent iodine; 20 percent vitamin B6; 35 percent vitamin C; plus thiamin, riboflavin, and zinc. That's quite a nutritional bargain.

Adding Fiber to Your Diet

1. Choose carbohydrates packaged in their natural coatings. Use brown rice instead of white; converted rice instead of instant. Use whole grain flour instead of white; unbleached flour instead of bleached. Use whole grain crackers, breads, and cereals. Read labels

and look for whole grain flour as a primary ingredient. Wheat flour is flour made from wheat. Often the most nutritious parts of the wheat have been removed. Whole wheat flour is made from the entire wheat kernel. It has more fiber and more nutrients.

2. Choose fresh vegetables with edible seeds and skins. Scrub, don't peel your carrots. Leave the skins on potatoes. Steam vegetables with peels on.

3. Choose fruits with edible seeds and skins. They can be raw or frozen or canned in unsweetened juice. Eat whole fruit. Drink less juice (especially important for diabetics since most fruit juices have a concentrated sugar content).

4. Legumes can sometimes cause gas, so start with the most easily digested kinds such as lentils, split peas, and lima beans. Work up to include navy, pinto, kidney, and black beans.

5. Use whole grains such as barley, bulgar (wheat), and kasha (buckwheat) as side dishes. Add wheat germ or wheat bran to meat loaf and meatballs. Make homemade corn bread and popcorn that is air popped or microwaved without added fat.

6. Be careful selecting cereals. As a general rule, the shorter the list of ingredients, the more nutritious the product. Look for a whole grain listed as the first ingredient, preferably with no added sugar or salt. Good choices include shredded wheat, oat bran (as a hot cereal), Wheatena, Nutri-Grain, Wheaties®, Total®, Quaker Oats® (not instant), and Grape Nuts.

7. Try to work up to 25 to 40 grams of fiber a day for each member of your family. Check with your child's dietitian about the best way to incorporate fiber into his diet.

8. Remember that soups are a great source of low-calorie, low-fat fiber and nutrition. Don't be limited by the ingredients listed. Add extra vegetables or grains and beans as you like.

THE EXCHANGE DIET

I first became familiar with the food exchange approach to dieting after my second child, Robin, was born. I needed to lose 18 pounds and tried the Weight Watchers diet. They use a system of food exchanges that is very easy to follow. When Brennan was diagnosed two years later, I had no problem implementing his diet plan—the exchanges seemed like old friends.

The Exchange Diet, developed by the American Dietetic Association and the American Diabetes Association, divides food into categories or classes, depending on the carbohydrate, protein, and fat content. Each type of food has approximately the same composition and caloric content as the others in its class. Therefore, one food can be exchanged or traded for another, which makes it easier to choose foods and make up balanced meals.

For example, starchy foods are generally listed under "Starch/Bread Exchanges." These foods include breads, pasta, starchy vegetables, dried peas and beans, and cereals. For each meal you choose from any of these exchange items to fulfill the amount of exchanges allowed in the diet plan. They share the following characteristics per serving:

Carbohydrate: 15 g

Protein: 3 g

Fat: trace

Calories: 80

The other food exchanges are:

Fruit Exchange

Carbohydrate: 15 g

Protein: 0

Fat: 0

Calories: 60

Milk Exchange (Skim)

  Carbohydrate: 12 g

  Protein: 8 g

  Fat: trace (for low-fat milk add 1 Fat Exchange, for whole milk
      add 2 Fat Exchanges)

  Calories: 90 (120 for low-fat, 150 for whole)

Meat Exchange (Lean)

  Carbohydrate: 0

  Protein: 7 g

  Fat: 3 g (For a medium-fat meat, add ½ Fat Exchange or 2 g; for
      a high-fat meat, add 1 Fat Exchange or 5 g)

  Calories: 55 (75 for medium-fat, 100 for high-fat)

Vegetable Exchange

  Carbohydrate: 5 g

  Protein: 2 g

  Fat: 0

  Calories: 25

Fat Exchange

  Carbohydrate: 0

  Protein: 0

  Fat: 5 g

  Calories: 45

The American Diabetes Association has a booklet entitled "Exchange Lists for Meal Planning" that lists the exchanges for most foods we eat. For brand-name foods, refer to Andrea Barrett's *The Diabetic's Brand-Name Food Exchange Handbook* (Philadelphia: Running Press, 1989). It lists calories and exchanges for 3,000 foods plus fast-food menus.

You can also calculate exchanges yourself. Use the label information and ask the following questions:

1. Which foods comprise this item?
2. What are the carbohydrate, protein, and fat grams?
3. Do the exchanges you compute total the ones listed on the label?

Let's use a Yoplait® Light yogurt as a model. It's nonfat and sweetened with NutraSweet. The ingredients are basically milk and fruit. The serving is 6 ounces at 90 calories. There are 14 grams of carbohydrates and 7 grams of protein, with no fat. One nonfat milk exchange is 12 grams carbohydrate, 8 grams protein, and 80 calories. The 10 calories and 2 grams carbohydrate left over most resemble ¼ fruit exchange, which is basically considered a free food at that small an amount. So Yoplait Light yogurt would count as a milk exchange.

When your child was diagnosed, you should have been given a diet plan based on the food exchanges. The plan was formulated on the basis of your child's weight and recommended daily intake of calories, protein, carbohydrates, and fats. Your child's insulin dosage is based primarily on the amount of carbohydrate that has been allowed.

Food exchanges help us become aware of the kinds and amounts of foods we are eating and feeding to our children. It's very important to educate yourself and your family about the value of good daily nutrition, but don't become too overzealous.

The idea is to be careful and responsible without adding additional stress to your lives. Become familiar with the recommended portion for an exchange by knowing what it looks like. For example, measure ½ cup of several different vegetables and see how much room is taken up on your child's plate. Compare a 3-ounce serving of chicken to the size of your child's fist so he can see how big it is. For a week or two, weigh and measure everything. You and your child will learn how to eyeball a portion to see if it's the right size. No one expects you and your child to drag measuring spoons and cups and scales around for the rest of your lives.

A doctor told me of one father whose controlling nature made his daughter's diabetes a nightmare. He made her follow her diet plan so exactly that he used to weigh and measure everything she ate. He even cut olives into quarters. When she became a teen she rebelled against his rigidity, ate anything she wanted, and jeopardized her health.

Reasonableness is vital. All of these methods of caring for a diabetic child are merely artificial approximations of a very complex natural system. No two days are alike. He uses differing amounts of energy from hour to hour; he grows at differing rates from week to week. Try to follow the Exchange Diet, but balance it with common sense. If your child is hungry, feed him. Use blood tests and insulin therapy along with advice from your diabetes professionals to keep blood sugar under good control.

Of all the parents I interviewed, none of them strictly used the Exchange Diet after the first year or so. The used a combination of good nutrition and moderation based on observation of how the Exchange Diet portions worked, as well as their own child's eating patterns and preferences. One mother found that when her daughter followed the exchange plan designed for her, she gained weight. They went on a low-fat, low-sugar diet together. In nine months the mother lost 96 pounds and her daughter lost 20 pounds.

I am not advising that you discard the Exchange Diet or its principles. You and your child will find ways to be responsible and reasonable about food intake and fit diabetes into your lives rather than make your lives fit diabetes.

THE GLYCEMIC INDEX

In the past, dietary recommendations were based on the chemical components of food. Now we have a method of judging how foods are handled in the body. There is a wide variation, for example, in biological responses to bread exchange foods such as rice, legumes, corn, pasta, and wheat. The system of judging these responses is called the Glycemic Index. It is devised by comparing the blood sugar rise caused by each food to the blood sugar rise caused by an equivalent amount of glucose. That results in a rating—100 being equal to a similar amount of glucose and then on down the scale.

You may have heard about the Glycemic Index and are wondering what it means to your diabetic child. The truth is, nobody is sure exactly what it means and diets are not undergoing drastic changes because of it. However, it indicates that nobody knew as much as was thought about the way food affects blood sugar.

The idea is that a food with a 50 rating raises blood sugar only half as much as one with a 100 rating. The lower the number, the lower the blood sugar rise. Here are some examples comparing similar types of food (read across):

Sweet potatoes–48	Instant potatoes–80	White potatoes–70
Beets–64	Carrots–92	Corn–59
Apples–39	Oranges–40	Bananas–62
Lentils–29	Baked beans–40	Green peas–51
Oatmeal–49	Shredded wheat–67	Corn flakes–80
Pasta–50	Brown rice–66	White rice–72
Peanuts–13	Potato chips–51	Mars bars–68
Skim milk–32	Yogurt–36	Ice cream–36

I know that some of this information may be confusing. For example, white potatoes raise blood sugar higher than ice cream, but from a nutritional standpoint, it would certainly be better to eat a baked potato every day than ice cream. There are also other factors to consider. The form of a food and the cooking process can affect glycemic response. Studies have shown that the more a food is processed, the quicker that food digests and the faster the rise in blood sugar. As an example, pureed vegetables raise blood sugar higher than chopped; chopped vegetables raise it higher than whole, and cooked vegetables raise it higher than raw.

In addition, the other foods eaten at a meal, the amount and type of fiber in the foods eaten, how much fat is in the food, the state of diabetes control, and the body's individual metabolism all have to be taken into consideration.

For these reasons, do not base food choices solely on the Glycemic Index. You can use it to help watch for foods that might send your child's blood sugar higher than desired. For example, we've learned that Chinese food and pizza send Brennan's blood sugar skyward. You can also use it to choose more foods with an index of 50 or lower to see how they affect postprandial blood sugar. By observation and blood testing, you and your child will learn which foods result in high blood tests.

You can obtain a copy of the Glycemic Index by calling Patient Information at the American Diabetes Association number listed in the Resources section.

EATING AWAY FROM HOME

For some parents, the thought of their diabetic child eating a meal while not under their watchful eye is frightening. If your child was diagnosed at a young age, there was a time when you could control everything he ate. That can't continue forever. Special occasions don't have to be a threat to good control; they just require planning. Diversionary tactics help, too. In this section, we'll look at eating at school and restaurants, and choosing fast-foods, plus parties, holidays, sports, and camping and provide ideas that will help you be flexible enough for any occasion.

School: To Take or Not to Take

School lunches can present a problem for a parent. If all the kids are eating the hot lunch sold at school, your child will probably want to be part of the pack. The problem is that school lunches are notoriously high in fat, sugar, and salt, as well as low in fiber—the opposite of what your child's meals should be.

It is important for your child to be a child first and a child who has diabetes second, and he is going to want to be like the other kids. If you can't get him to take a sack lunch every day, try getting a copy of the monthly school lunch menu and sending special "treats" to substitute when some of the foods served must be completely avoided.

It's good to let your child take some responsibility for his diabetes as early as possible. That includes his making some poor choices now and then. You two might have discussed the lunch menus and decided which days the substitutions were needed. But your child decided to eat the dessert on one of those days anyway, instead of the apple you packed. After-school blood tests will show the results of eating the dessert. You then have an opportunity to discuss how sugary foods affect his blood sugar and what better choices he might make next time.

You can also talk with cafeteria personnel about the lunches. Sometimes they are very helpful and will pull the dessert or canned fruit from the tray, thereby eliminating some of the temptation.

The lunch you send to school can be packed with anything from sandwiches to soups and stews, salads, cup-up veggies, and fruit. The possibilities are endless when you have the appropriate containers. Soups and stews stay warm in individual-serving thermos jars. Tupperware® makes a lunch pail that has containers to hold sandwiches, drinks, and moist foods like fruit salad. We used to put a Tupperware cup of a sugar-free drink (like Crystal Light) in the freezer overnight. The next morning, we snapped the lid on the frozen liquid. By noon it had thawed but was still cold.

You and your child can make a list of lunch menus and special treats to send from home. This gives your child a sense of control over his diet and gives you an idea of what he likes. Make sure it includes foods for each of the exchanges.

You will need to have a discussion, preferably face to face, with each of your child's teachers about your child's dietary limits at snack times and at parties, as well as how to treat insulin reactions. The parameters for these discussions and lists of supplies will be presented in chapter 6.

Restaurants: The Rules of Order

Eating out with a diabetic child doesn't have to be a problem. It just requires some planning and common sense. First of all, be sure you take the insulin and test equipment with you. I don't even want to think about all the times we got to the restaurant and realized we'd left them sitting on the kitchen counter. One time, we were thirty minutes from the house and had to find a pharmacy on Sunday night. We drove around for fifteen minutes and got there just as the pharmacist was leaving and pleaded with him to sell us two bottles of insulin. By the time we got the shot done and returned to the restaurant, everyone else was halfway through dinner. Not our best night out!

Timing the shot and the arrival of dinner can be a problem, especially if dinner is delayed. Try giving the shot just before or after you order, depending on how high or low the blood test is. If your child starts to feel low because the service is slow, ask the waiter to quickly bring a glass of orange juice. You can also prevent this situation by asking the waiter to bring your child's milk to the table immediately.

On several occasions, Brennan ordered diet sodas and was served sugared ones. One trick, other than a taste test, is to use urine test strips such as Diastix. Just as they will indicate sugar in the urine, they will indicate sugar in a soft drink. Or you can use a professional, like my younger son Robin, who can identify a diet drink at twenty paces!

Watch out for hidden fats. Fried foods, cream sauces, salad dressings, gravies, and mayonnaise are the primary culprits. Ask how a dish is prepared. Try to choose restaurants that support low-fat eating; many now offer dishes prepared according to American Heart Association guidelines. Most restaurants also carry low-fat milk. If the portions are too large, ask for a doggie bag and take the rest home. Fresh fruit or a small serving of ice cream are good dessert choices.

Use eating out as an opportunity for your child to make choices based on his diet plan. If he is allowed three starch/bread exchanges for dinner, he can figure how many dinner rolls to eat and still be able to eat his rice or potato. Giving your child some choice in these decisions will help develop a sense of control and responsibility toward diabetes.

Fast Foods

Sooner or later you have to deal with fast foods and the establishments that offer them. Fast food is far from nutritionally ideal, but eating it occasionally is not going to harm your child. The key, once again, is moderation. There are good reasons for this.

Be aware that most of the foods served are high in fat, sodium, and calories. For example, Burger King's chicken sandwich has 42 g of fat, 775 mg of sodium, and 690 calories. At calories per gram of fat, that's 388 calories or over 50 percent from fat! These foods are also woefully short on fiber.

In a step in the right direction, many fast-food restaurants now offer salad bars and baked potatoes. Be sure to calculate the dressings and toppings, which add fat and calories. You can try bringing packets of a favorite low-calorie dressing with you instead of eating their fat-laden versions.

Try to get your child to stick to simple fare—a hamburger instead of a Big Mac™, a small order of fries, and a diet soda. A meal like that would register approximately 4 bread, 2 medium-fat meat, and 2 or 3 fat exchanges.

You should familiarize yourself with the nutritional breakdown of fast foods. I suggest you get a copy of *Fast Food Facts,* by Marian Franz. It gives the calories, carbohydrate, protein, fat, sodium, and exchanges for food served at twenty-six fast-food chains. There is advice about fast-food dining and a list of foods to definitely avoid.

The Fast Food Checker, published by Lite Styler, is pocket-sized so you can easily carry it in your wallet. It lists all the above information and the cholesterol content. Depending on your child's age, you can discuss this information in greater or lesser detail and make informed decisions. Both of these books are available from the Sugarfree Center listed in the Resources section.

Some chains are offering healthier choices. El Pollo Loco's® chicken is low in fat and cholesterol and not as bad as others in the sodium department. The tide is turning in favor of healthier choices and we should see more restaurants offering them in the future.

Party Time

Party time requires extra thought and planning. If the party is in your home, you can control what foods are served. You don't have to serve candy to have a successful party for kids. Chips and dip, cut-up carrots and celery, small boxes of raisins, and an ice cream cake will be gobbled up.

One mother serves do-it-yourself ice cream cones. Her child's is prepared with sugarless ice cream; everyone else gets regular ice cream decorated with sprinkles. Then they put a candle in each cone and stand around the birthday girl to sing "Happy Birthday."

I use sugar-free drinks for punch or serve a variety of regular and diet soft drinks. We make exercise and games a substantial part of the party. One year, we had everyone bring tennis shoes and we had a big free-for-all soccer game on a tennis court. We had prizes for the winning team. Then we had the teams play each other in Junior Trivia and bingo. It was a great party.

If you're serving lunch, make stacks of oven-baked chicken legs and tuna or peanut butter and low-sugar jam sandwiches. Put out bowls of seedless green grapes, strawberries, and plums. Believe it or not, kids will eat food that is good for them at a party!

If the party is not held in your home, how you handle it depends on your child's age. A teenager will not want Mom or Dad interfering in his social life, but with a younger child, you will want to call the hosts and see what foods will be served. You can then discuss the choices beforehand with your child. A small piece of cake without icing counts as approximately 2 bread and 1 fat exchanges. A small scoop of ice cream counts as 1 bread, 2 fat.

I got a letter a few years ago from a nine-year-old girl who wanted a recipe for a sugarless cake for her birthday party. Her best friend had diabetes and the girl's mother never let her go to parties where "bad" foods were served. What a shame to restrict a child's life so unnecessarily! Her friend could easily have had a small piece of cake or a scoop of ice cream and worked it into her diet plan, or could have taken a little extra insulin. If she had a high blood sugar two hours after eating, she could have consulted with her doctor and used a combination of insulin and exercise to bring the blood sugar down to normal levels.

This overprotective mom could have used the policy of a mother who wrote to me recently. She knows that her daughter can eat a small piece of cake without it raising her blood sugar by much. She incorporates the cake into her exchange plan, then tries to discourage her from munching on chips, nuts, and other high-calorie treats. Before the party, she lets her daughter choose what she would rather have, some of the treats or the cake. Her little girl most often chooses the cake. Mom also brings a sugar-free drink in a thermos, along with carrot and celery sticks or sugar-free Jell-O cubes, so that they are available.

There are several approaches to use that make allowance for the extra calories your child might be ingesting. One is to give extra insulin to cover the treats. A word of caution from Mary Ann Robnett: This suggestion can be easily abused! If the party coincides with mealtime, use allotted exchanges from that meal and also use physical activity to balance the extra calories. (Exercise should not be initiated if the blood sugar level is over 300.) Discuss which choice is best suited to your child with your diabetes adviser.

Your child can enjoy the party and still maintain reasonable control. Moderation and planning are the keys. A party is a good learning opportunity for your child. He can learn to make appropriate choices and be responsible for his diabetes, while seeing that diabetes control can be flexible enough to allow him to be like other kids.

Holidays: Gobble, Gobble

Holidays mean food and plenty of it. It's not an easy time for someone on a controlled diet plan. The same discipline and planning that underlies the rest of your child's year is essential during the holidays. Again, your support and your own attitude will make a big difference. If you feel your child is being "cheated" out of enjoying the holidays because his diet is restricted, your child will pick up on your feelings even if you don't verbalize them. Your acceptance and accommodation of his diabetes is more important than anything else. We'll delve into this subject more fully later, but for now let's look at ways to take the stress out of diabetes and holiday eating.

No matter what holiday we discuss, at least some of the foods that are served must fit your child's diet plan. That may require rethinking Grandma's sweet potato pie. Is it loaded with sugar and butter? Is there a way you could modify it without the rest of the family saying you've ruined it? Perhaps, after thinking it through, you'll decide to make a second, sugar-free pie so that your child has an alternative. Then it's nice if several other family members also have a piece of the second pie as a show of support (choosing, of course, the family members most likely to be sincerely supportive).

For Halloween, use a negotiation approach. You needn't ban your child from trick-or-treating. Make an agreement beforehand that nothing will be eaten until the bag comes home. Separate the candy from the "OK" goodies such as apples, raisins, sugarless gum, or cash. Trade the candy for money and a trip to the toy store or replace the candy with a sugar-free kind. You can also save the sugared treats for insulin reactions. Another suggestion is to have your child collect money for diabetes research. JDF has had a successful campaign at Halloween called "Treat a Kid Who Can't Have a Treat."

For Easter baskets, use colored eggs, sugarless gum and candy, and little toys or favors.

For Christmas and Thanksgiving, contact your doctor or dietitian to discuss either increasing the insulin dosage or sticking closely to the diet plan. Some parents allow a small taste of each dish to avoid isolating their child.

Try to make the holidays a social time to share one another's company, not an occasion defined only by food. Play parlor games together or read a holiday story. It's a good idea to include some exercise—a broom hockey game, an interfamily basketball tournament, even a table tennis tournament will get people on their feet and moving and give everyone, including your diabetic child, a chance to work off some calories.

Occasional departures from a diabetic diet are not going to harm your child if the basic, daily control is good. Diabetes is a train that takes you for a lifelong ride. Giving a child no leeway can result in rebellion. In reality, any food can be eaten by a diabetic person. There is nothing that's a "never." A small taste, as part of a meal containing fat and fiber, is a good alternative to a pig-out sneaked when no one is looking. There is room in your child's life for mistakes. Besides, there will be a point where you'll no longer be able to control what your child chooses to eat. By then, you want to have demonstrated to your child that diabetes is a workable part of his life. To help make your cooking life easier, see *Kids, Food, and Diabetes* in the Resources section.

Camping

A family camping trip is a great source of togetherness, as well as providing relaxation and exercise. All that increased activity means increased need for calories. The caloric output can rise from 2,000 to 3,000 calories a day because of hiking, bicycling, and other activities. One father found that when the family was hiking, it was necessary to give his daughter one fruit exchange every half-hour. Discuss adjusting your child's food intake with your health professional.

Choose a campsite where medical help is available locally, but be prepared anyway. Take two bottles of each insulin your child uses with plenty of extra syringes. The extra insulin can be kept in a cooler along with juice, diet sodas, and regular sodas. Be sure to take glucagon (it does not have to be refrigerated) and the appropriate syringe. Also have glucose tablets and/or liquid glucose for reactions. Cans of juice, boxes of raisins and other dried fruit, and packages of cheese and crackers are also good to keep handy at all times.

Blood testing becomes even more valuable as schedules change, so take everything you need and more. Divide the supplies into a few different locations. Make certain they are well padded and out of direct sunlight. If you go hiking, take whatever you need with you plus a little extra, in case the hike takes longer than you thought. Everything will probably go smoothly, but you'll feel much better knowing you have everything you need.

Talk with your diabetes professional before you go. Make sure your child has a medical identification bracelet or pendant on at all times in case you are separated.

The Sporting Life

There are two ways to attend a sporting event, as a spectator and as a participant. If your child is participating, there are several factors of which to be aware. One is the time of the event and which insulin will be working at that time (as discussed in chapter 3). If it's the middle of the morning, the Regular will be at work and you may need to give extra food and/or less insulin. If the game's in the afternoon, the NPH is working. If you're in doubt, consult the doctor about what adjustments need to be made.

One father had a problem with his son's very early sports schedule. The question was, when your child has to rise at 5 A.M. for a game, do you give a normal breakfast shot or withhold insulin until the regular breakfast time? When his son took his breakfast shot at 5 A.M., he had reactions during the event. It also threw his whole day's schedule off because his NPH peaked at 2 or 3 in the afternoon. Then he ran high blood sugars the next morning. The solution was to give a "mini" insulin dose when the son woke up and let him eat a small meal at least half an hour before the activity. The father found he had low-normal to normal blood sugars by following this routine. After the game, he'd have his morning shot and regular breakfast.

Another factor is adrenaline, which is released in times of stress and causes a rise in blood sugar. Each child's body responds differently to excitement and anxiety. Keeping close track of blood sugar will give you and your child the information you need to decide (with your doctor) what to do about adjusting the insulin dose on game days.

It's always a good idea to test blood sugar before strenuous activity and provide extra food as needed. Carry fruit juice, Gatorade, glucose tablets, and liquid glucose. Your dietitian can provide additional ideas. Your child should carry a glucose source with him at all times. Be sure coaches and gym teachers are aware that your child has diabetes and know how to recognize and treat reactions.

Being a spectator is more passive and merely means having to deal with all the less-than-healthy foods sold at sporting events. The foods served there are almost all high in fat—hamburgers, hot dogs, fries, chips, peanuts. Try to limit the amount and, if it's at mealtime, consider bringing some carrot sticks and fresh fruit to add some good nutrition. Again, if it's a once-in-a-while thing, don't make a big deal. Just try to stay within the allotted food exchanges if possible.

There are many feelings that can accompany being on a restricted diet. Food is the most visible issue of having diabetes. You can assist your child to develop a healthy attitude about the restrictions demanded by diabetes. For example, if your child doesn't want to go into a long explanation, he can respond to questions about why he doesn't eat a certain food with "I don't care for it." If he honestly didn't like it, he wouldn't feel isolated or strange about not eating it, would he? You can show him that just because he makes certain choices does not mean he has to feel different or bad about himself.

This example brings us to the issues of what it feels like to have diabetes and what it feels like to care for a child with diabetes. Up to now we have examined the practical aspects of caring for your child. These elements are tangible; we can weigh and measure them. The other facet of caring for your child is the manner in which you assist his emotional and psychological acceptance of diabetes, which is as important as the tests and shots. Just as vital is the way you accept and manage your feelings about your child having diabetes.

The next chapter will help you understand the way your child may view having diabetes and how his feelings may affect his behavior. The following chapter is about your feelings and responsibilities as a parent.

5

Lousy Ketchup

Living with diabetes is not simply a matter of balancing insulin, food, and exercise. As parents, we must also help our children balance their feelings.

A young child can sometimes have a much different view of everything that is going on. I remember asking Brennan, several years after his diagnosis, what he most remembered about his stay at the hospital at that time. I thought he would recount being frightened and how he had screamed when the nurse had taken blood from his arm. Or perhaps he would tell me of his confusion concerning all the strange happenings and changes from that time forward. What did he recall from the six most painful days of our life together, those first days of diabetes? He remembered, "They had lousy ketchup." I viewed those days as ones that shattered the context of our lives, and what did my son most remember? That the dietetic ketchup was "lousy"!

This chapter is concerned with the way your child views the world, gives you clues about what his feelings might be, and discusses how you and your child can successfully handle his feelings about having diabetes. We'll look at the skills that contribute to good parenting. Along with an overview of some of the patterns of a child's development, we'll examine the feelings most likely to be experienced by children who have diabetes—denial, anger, fear, rebellion, isolation—and deal with specific problems which arise at each major state of childhood: toddlerhood, the grade school years, and the teens. I'll also provide examples of how to remedy difficulties that threaten your child's psychological and emotional well-being as well as his blood sugar control.

A CHILD'S DEVELOPMENT

A child's perception of the world is limited in much the same way that his physical abilities are limited. As his body grows, so grows his understanding. In addition, there is a rhythmic pattern to a child's psychological and emotional development. There are periods of happiness and security countered by periods of disruption. These are known as stages of equilibrium and disequilibrium. These patterns are evident as we look at some of the general characteristics of each age. Knowing these patterns can help you become more aware of the additional difficulties diabetes may present for your child.

These ages and descriptions are, of course, approximate and your child should not be measured against them. Each child is an individual and exemplifies these growth patterns in his own way. They are to be used as a tool to help you be more sensitive to nonverbal communication and to have more realistic expectations of your child's capabilities.

The First Five Years

In the first two years of life, a child is operating on a very basic level. These are the years when a basic sense of trust is formulated. That trust centers on whether or not the infant's needs are met. The child learns if this world is a safe place. "Am I fed when I'm hungry? Am I comforted when I'm unhappy? Am I loved? Am I lovingly touched?"

The answers to these questions give an infant a foundation that will color his whole life. There can be discomfort, there can be shots and blood tests, but what really makes a difference is the way these events are handled. Since an infant doesn't understand words, communication rests largely on physical contact. Is there love and comfort after the shot or blood test? Are there soothing tones in the words spoken? The atmosphere and empathy you give your baby matter much more than the temporary distress. Having to inflict pain and discomfort is very difficult, even though you know it is for your child's good. Be assured that it will not damage your child or his relationship with you. What is most important is that you communicate your love and respect for this little person who is in your care.

Even though I stress the physical aspects of comforting your child, don't underestimate the power of unspoken attitudes and thoughts. We've all met people who say one thing and clearly convey something else. My father liked the saying, "What you are shouts so loudly I can't hear what you're saying!" The point is, if you're frustrated and feeling angry, your child will sense it. Infants are very adept at picking up on the feelings of their parents. We'll talk more about our feelings as parents in the next chapter.

When a child reaches toddlerhood his main issue is independence. It's a very powerful stage of life, also known as the first adolescence. The toddler is just beginning to develop and express his sense of self as well as differentiating that self from his mother. The king of egocentrics, he believes that he is the center of the universe. Cause and effect mean little. Everything exists for the moment. He finds it difficult to handle more than one situation at a time. Because he thinks he is the origin of all actions, a child of his age may also have a strong sense of guilt. He may think he causes everything that happens. He may view pain and illness as a punishment.

This first adolescence encompasses children two to five years old. The two-year-old generally feels sure of himself as he uses language to make his needs known, yet he can't fully express his fears and desires and can be easily frustrated—hence the phrase "terrible twos." During this year of being two, he can become demanding and inflexible, wanting to make all the decisions himself. Since he has no basis by which to choose alternatives, those decisions can be very difficult. It can be an age of often violent emotions.

At three, resistance changes to conformity and cooperation; it is an easier time because the child is better able to express himself. People are important to him and he may enjoy sharing. At three and a half he can, once again, enter a time of insecurity and disequilibrium. Lake of coordination sometimes characterizes this age, as well as jealousy.

Four is an age best described as "out of bounds." Everything is overboard. Your child can be loud and silly or full of anger. He may defy his parents or use language to shock them. He loves make-believe; his imagination is boundless. He is testing himself and the world around him. It is a brash age.

At four and a half, he may begin to pull back a little and show more concern for what is real. He loves to discuss things in detail, and likes being shown how things work. Your child is improving his control and perfecting his skills. He also handles frustration a little better.

Five is an age of balance. The five-year-old is reliable, stable, and well adjusted. He likes to be instructed and to get permission. He wants to do what's right.

The Middle Years

Grade school years are a period of adjustment to the world outside the family home. Your child is subjected to expectations from teachers and peers, and acceptance by one's peers becomes very important. The problem of feeling different is not easy at this age. On the one hand, you want to reassure your child that he is not "different," yet adjusting to having diabetes means accepting the "differentness" and being comfortable with his uniqueness.

At the same time that your child is struggling to adjust to the outside world and peer pressure, the alternating rhythm of development continues. The six-year-old, much like the two-and-a-half-year-old, can be an emotional extremist who wants to be the center of his world. At seven, he may be more withdrawn, more likely to complain and demand. He may think that people are picking on him or that they don't like him.

Eight-year-olds tend to meet the world head on, filled with enthusiasm and energy. The child expects much of himself and his relationships with others. Nine is more self-contained, self-sufficient, more inclined to worry and be anxious. Nine also is an age very concerned with pain and discomfort.

Ten is often one of the nicest ages, characterized by cheerful obedience. Your child can be very satisfied with parents, teachers, and the world in general. Eleven tends to be a time to be more assertive, curious, and sociable. On the go, the child talks and talks and may seem to be hungry all the time. He may be intense and subject to variable moods. His whole being is in a process of growth and reorganization.

Twelve is less insistent, more reasonable and companionable. Your preteen is in a stage of widening awareness, trying to grow up. His peer group is very important in shaping his attitudes and interests. Increased self-insight and self-control, along with a greater sense of perspective, attend this age.

The "Terrible" Teens

The teen years are much the same as the "terrible twos," marked by similar striving for independence and individuality, though on a more complex level. And the same rhythmic personality changes based on general patterns of equilibrium and disequilibrium continue to take place as the child grows to young adulthood.

The thirteen-year-old may withdraw a bit. Not always communicative anyway, he may have spells of silence. He can worry a great deal. It is a time of taking in, mulling over. He is not retreating from reality, he is probing and reflecting. He becomes more discriminating about the friends he chooses and the way he looks.

Fourteen can be more robust and expressive. Filled with self-assurance, the teen seems better able to enjoy himself and his friends. He also may enjoy a better relationship with his parents, based on mutual understanding and respect. He may be anxious to be popular and sensitive about being different.

Fifteen becomes more thoughtful and the teen may even seem indifferent. He is frugal with his physical energy and may be considered lazy or, at least, tired. Concerned with precision, he makes an effort to find just the right words to express himself. His moods are probably not as intense as they were at thirteen. Development at this point is marked by increasing self-awareness, independence, and loyalty to home and school.

Sixteen is self-assured. The teen has achieved a sense of independence, often has many friends, and usually prefers their company to the company of his family. He is more aware of the future, the long run, and has strong feelings about college, marriage, and career. Sixteen is generally well balanced and is more willing to see another person's view.

GOOD PARENTING SKILLS

I'm sure you agree that being a parent is the most important and demanding job that we will ever have. It is a job for which we have received no formal training. Our training has been by osmosis—we parent basically the same way we were parented, unless we have the courage and energy to unlearn and rethink some of our childhood lessons.

The difficulty of being a parent is heightened when diabetes enters the picture. Now there is an enlarged sense of mortality and potential loss compounded by a need for increased watchfulness and discipline. In a word, "Yikes!"

Our acceptance of this challenge, diabetes, is the first hurdle we must overcome in order to help our children. Acceptance, in its largest sense, means being willing to hear and to tell the truth. We need to be willing to hear what our children have to say and what they feel about having diabetes.

Most of us have been raised with at least some denial of our feelings. Sometimes, without thinking, we pass that denial on to our children. I remember when my first husband and I had to tell our boys that we were getting divorced. I asked a counselor for advice. He told me, "Don't tell them it will be okay. That's a lie. It will never be okay for them. Tell them it will be difficult. Tell them you love them and will help them through it in every way you can. Just don't tell them it will be okay."

Isn't that exactly what we would like to do with our children about their diabetes? Reassure them? Tell them it will be okay? Yet, we must remember not to lie and to acknowledge the truth when told from the child's perspective. Your child cries after his shot. Perhaps your instinct is to say, "Now that wasn't so bad!" Yet the truth for your child is that, for that moment, it *was* bad. You help your child accept the "bad" by your accepting it.

There are areas of emotional adjustment and parenting skills that will prove valuable as you help your child learn to live successfully with diabetes: your expectations, your listening skills, building your child's self-esteem, and setting appropriate limits.

Adjusting Your Expectations

I believe that diabetes is much harder on a parent than it is on the child at this stage. You know what diabetes is and what it can do. Paul Madden of the Joslin Diabetes Center in Boston has seen repeatedly that parents worry much more about their children's diabetes than their children do. Your own reaction to your child's having diabetes may be gut-level fear. You may feel that if you're not at your child's side every minute, something terrible will happen that no one but you can handle. At the same time, your child's growth and development is geared toward independence and autonomy.

One of the thoughts that may come to a parent's mind is that diabetes is going to ruin her child's emotional and psychological life. It will change it, but there's no reason your child can't grow to be as well adjusted as any other person.

This was not always thought to be the case. Health professionals used to be of the opinion that chronically ill children would automatically have psychological problems. That's just not true, according to experts such as Dr. Jonathan Kellerman, co-founder and former director of the Psychosocial Program at Children's Hospital, Los Angeles. In a study he conducted with his associates, adolescents with diabetes, cancer, and cystic fibrosis were compared with a matched set of teenagers without any illnesses. The tests were based on standardized psychological measures. Both groups were found to be basically the same. In each group, most of them were well adjusted and some had problems. So, the fact that your child has physical problems does not necessarily mean that he will have emotional problems. He can grow up to be as stable and fulfilled as anyone else.

I believe that what each of us becomes is based on what we've brought with us into this world and what comes our way as we spend our lives here. Diabetes is only one influence in your child's life. I know it can feel as if it's going to pull you under at times, but it can also make your child stronger and more disciplined, with a sensitivity to others that will remain a positive asset of his personality.

Diabetes does present a powerful challenge. One of the major psychological issues of childhood is learning control and mastery of one's life. (I know I'm still working on it!) Diabetes adds an additional element to that control issue.

Juvenile diabetes is actually one of the most difficult diseases because of all the demands that it makes on a child's behavior. Many illnesses are passive ones. You receive treatment, you take your medication. Your doctor makes decisions, you follow directions. Diabetes places almost all of the required care in the patient's lap. It necessitates learning to be your own doctor and demands constant awareness and discipline.

Think of how difficult it is for most adults to give up smoking or stay on a strict diet for a long time. Yet we ask an eight- or nine-year-old to stick to his diet, test, and shot regimen every hour of every day. Clearly, that requires a level of self-control that a young child has not yet developed.

I recently heard of a doctor who recommended an experiment for parents designed to help them understand what their children might be feeling. He suggested that they follow a strict diet plan similar to the child's, plus give themselves blood tests and injections of saline solution whenever the child did. Most of the parents couldn't stay on that program for more than a few days. It helped them understand the feelings that their children experience and to adjust their expectations accordingly.

Listening

In dealing with your child's emotions, it is important to understand that children are not mature enough to identify or clearly express their feelings. They need our help. We've had many more years to develop the tools and experience to deal with feelings.

The starting point in dealing with your child's emotions is knowing how to actively listen. Active listening is a technique used to feed back to the speaker what he was actually expressing about his feelings, not what you wish he was feeling.

It is a wonderful thing to be listened to, to be acknowledged, and to know that what we're thinking and feeling has value. This feeling of being valued first appears in the eyes and actions of our mothers and fathers. By their manner of treating us we form our way of seeing ourselves as well as our view of the world. A person's worldview is a fundamental key to all he does. It determines his perspective and way of functioning in the world. Extending yourself to understand the way your child sees things is an act of love. It is also hard work.

Your child doesn't talk to you on schedule. Sometimes he doesn't say a thing for a long time and then one question, lovingly heard and thoughtfully answered, can open up a long discussion. Sometimes these issues are painful to discuss or very difficult to articulate. Your child may feel guilty, believing he has caused his diabetes and given this terrible burden to his parents. He may be holding back a story about peer pressure or cruelty because he knows it will bother his parents. He may be afraid he will die. Listening and validating his feelings can help tremendously.

As an example, your child says, "I hate my shots. I hate you." You might respond, "I know you hate your shots. It's very difficult to take shots every day. I see that you're very angry with me because I give you the shots. I wish I didn't have to do it."

Validating means acknowledging, letting your child know that he has a right to his feelings. Have you ever been really angry and had someone keep nagging you to "calm down, calm down"? I don't know about you, but that makes me even angrier. If I feel angry, I will calm down when I'm ready. I feel I am entitled to my feelings. So is your child.

Many of us have been taught that certain feelings are "not nice." The problem with trying to ignore so-called "bad feelings" is that they don't go away just because we refuse to look at them. (Actually, a more constructive approach is to accept that no feelings are "bad.") Keeping feelings locked away can actually make them seem bigger and more destructive than they are. Shining a little light on them reveals them to be temporary bits of emotional energy that will change as time passes.

There are several specific techniques you can use to help your child express himself:

1. Paraphrase. Use slightly different words to reflect back to your child the message you just received. Your child says she doesn't want to attend a slumber party because it's a hassle to give herself a shot, and also because of all the junk food. You reply, "It sounds like it's embarrassing to have to give yourself your test and shot with all your friends there. And it must be really hard to resist all the food." Your child now knows that you've understood her feelings. If not, she can correct your interpretation of her remarks.

2. Elaborate. It's not easy for a child to clearly express his emotions. Help your child understand the varying degrees of an emotion by expanding his description. When your child says he is "mad," you can feed back words like "irritated, annoyed, or furious." Your child can then develop more skill at accurately expressing himself.

3. Wonder If. You may notice that your child is feeling a particular way but has not said anything. You now assist your child by

acknowledging his apparent emotional state. "I wonder if you're angry because your brother has a candy bar and you don't?" This gives your child permission to express a difficult emotion, as well as providing a model for expressing it.

4. Wait and Ask. Our natural inclination as parents is to want to offer solutions to our children when they are having trouble. This may be interpreted by your child as not listening or caring about the feelings expressed: "You just don't understand!" Try to wait before offering a solution. First ask, "What do you think would help?" This conveys your trust in your child's ability to solve problems and your respect for his opinion. If your child has no ideas, you can then suggest that you both think about it. If your child asks for a suggestion, try giving your opinion as if it were only one of the possible solutions. Your child may also come up with a good solution, and it will help him feel very good about himself.

5. Accept Ambivalence. Your child may have conflicted feelings about an issue; help him identify those emotions without demanding that he instantly resolve the conflict. For example, your child wants to begin giving his own injection and feel proud of himself for being so grown-up, yet he's truly afraid of doing it. Allow the impasse to exist; support his time of indecision. "It must be tough to start giving your own injections. Don't worry. You'll do it when you're ready. There's no hurry."

6. Check Again. No matter how well your child seems to be doing, you need to keep checking to see how he feels. You may have explained something once, but he may have forgotten or misinterpreted it. Children can take things quite literally. One boy had nightmares about bugs and monsters for a week after having the flu. After much probing, his mother discovered he had overheard her say that he "had a bug."

7. Play Therapy. For a child who is too young to verbalize his feelings, play therapy can be a valuable tool. Pounding wood, working with clay, drawing or painting or acting out with dolls and puppets can be creative outlets for your child's feelings. One mother told me that her son, Adam, has decided that his Ninja Turtle, Raphael, has diabetes. Likewise, when Brennan first came home from the hospital after being diagnosed, he decided that his favorite doll, Joey, also had diabetes. He gave Joey shots until the newness of it all wore off. I think it helped him feel a sense of control by playing the role of the shot giver, not just the shot receiver.

By encouraging your child to talk about his emotions, and by listening and validating what he feels, you have the opportunity to show your child that all of his feelings are a valuable part of him and worthy of loving attention.

Building Self-Esteem

Building your child's self-esteem is one of the most important tasks of parenting. We want our child to feel good about who he is and what he does. One way of achieving that goal is by encouraging your child's sense of self-sufficiency in all the areas of life. Just as your child needs to take responsibility for his homework, he needs to be allowed to gradually take responsibility for his diabetes.

A child's body image can contribute significantly to his self-concept. Getting diabetes can alter your child's body image. The trick is to use the diabetes to increase self-esteem whenever possible. Focus on the positive and praise your child for taking responsibility. Encourage your child to feel competent about his ability to handle diabetes. When the blood sugar readings are not as controlled as desired, don't blame or judge but work together with your doctor or educator to discover the causes and make adjustments as needed.

As one mother advises, "Use diabetes as a tool to build your child's self-esteem because of his ability to make wise choices, comprehend technical information, follow complex directions, and know the principles of good nutrition. After all, how many eight-year-olds discuss grams of fat and calories in their diets?"

Developing confidence concerning diabetes management starts from the earliest ages. Help your child find a way to verbalize low blood sugar symptoms as early as possible. It might be "I feel funny" or "I'm low." One two-and-a-half-year-old has taken it one step farther. If she feels hungry, which may be a sign of low blood sugar, she knows her mom will test her blood. She merely tells her mom, "Let's do a blood sugar" and climbs up to the kitchen counter to get the blood testing machine. She then does her own finger prick and puts the test strip in the machine.

Even very young children will want to participate in some aspect of their care. The main consideration is to allow your child to proceed at his own pace. You can suggest that he help and then let the decision be his. As a reference, most children take over doing their tests and shots by them-selves (with supervision) usually at nine years of age.

Self-esteem evolves from feeling good about ourselves and how we manage our lives. It is the foundation of an authentic person. Allowing a child who has diabetes the room to be responsible, to make mistakes, and to learn from those mistakes is essential to the development of a positive self-image.

As one mother wrote: "Let your child be who he was created to be. Give of yourself without trying to take his difficulties away from him. They are rightfully his. Show a willingness to compromise even if you don't feel like doing that. Support his choices, when he makes them, knowing they will always be his to make. Most of all, praise him for his effort. Be ready to step back and let him shine."

Setting Limits

It is so difficult to watch something disturb or hurt our children, and diabetes certainly does both. It is natural to feel sorry for your child. You may want to compensate, to bend over backward to make life less trying for him. It is valuable to keep in mind just how easily your desire to compensate can be turned to your and your child's disadvantage.

Even though he has diabetes, you must continue to set limits and demand that rules be followed. The key is to ask yourself, "If my child didn't have diabetes, would I let him do this?" If the answer is no, then don't let him do it. It is not your job to make life as easy as possible for your child. Our job as parents is to love and protect our children and to equip them for all that life will throw their way. Yes, they've had this terrible thing called diabetes come into their lives, but now we must do all we can to encourage them to live with the challenge it represents without self-pity or excuses. They must learn to live their lives with forethought and discipline, within the limits imposed by diabetes.

As one father puts it, "Love your child, but never let him feel that you love him more than you would if he didn't have diabetes. Treat him as normally as possible. If he's out of line, he's out of line: diabetes or no diabetes. Don't ever let diabetes become an excuse!"

Within the limitations imposed by diabetes, there are many choices to be made. For example, your child's shot and blood test must be done, yet he can choose how he wants to assist. Depending on his age, he can choose the site, prick his finger, turn on the machine, or load the syringe. You can encourage him to decorate his equipment with stickers. If he's low and must eat something, don't ask if he wants to eat because a "no" is unacceptable. Instead, give him a choice: "Do you want to eat ____ or ____ or ____?" Always try to provide some choices within the structure of the routine that must be accomplished.

There's the possibility that at some time your child may try to use his diabetes to manipulate you. One mother provided a good example when she wrote that she wasn't sure what to do when her daughter called from school to say that she didn't feel well. Mom was sure she'd been a "chump" on occasion. Plenty of kids, with and without diabetes, try the "I Don't Feel Well on Test Day" trick.

If her daughter had blood testing equipment at school, she could have determined if she had low blood sugar and then eaten a snack to bring it back to normal. If there was no equipment at school, mom could have offered to drive over and test her, asking her if she was absolutely sure her diabetes was causing the problem. If not, and there were no other symptoms, such as fever, she should have asked her daughter to be very specific about what was bothering her and dealt with it as she would any nondiabetic child. A slightly elevated blood sugar is not an excuse to miss school. Dr. Rood suggests that if there's no fever or vomiting, and the blood sugar is under 400, the child goes to school. By following these guidelines, this mom would teach her daughter that having diabetes is not an excuse for missing school.

One mother told me of the time her daughter came running into the house asking for money to buy something from the ice cream truck. It was not long before dinner, she hadn't yet had her shot, and it would raise her blood sugar. All these were very good reasons why this mom had to say no, yet she felt terrible. She felt she was denying her child the chance to be like all the other kids. She once again felt the sadness of her child's having diabetes, that her young life was now so limited. A while later, he daughter came back in and announced that, since it was just before dinner, none of the other kids had been able to have ice cream either. That mom learned a valuable lesson: Don't project sadness and guilt into setting limits. The other mothers were setting limits based on what they thought was best for their children and so was she.

One mother noted that her effort to be very matter-of-fact and not be manipulated by her daughter has paid off. "I knew that if I let Kaitlin know how hard it was for me to prick her fingers and give her shots, she would soon learn that she could use tests and shots as a bargaining chip. Now, we have the least behavioral problems around testing and shots, most likely because of our consistency."

I speak of the importance of setting limits because I know how vital it is. I was not very good at it when Brennan was younger; I felt so bad about his having diabetes that it was difficult for me to appropriately discipline him. I know now that that approach didn't help him learn the art of self-discipline. Confusing affection and security with permissiveness and failure to set limits won't help your child either.

Extra Help

Being a good and effective parent is a demanding job. There may be occasions when it seems overwhelming. Please don't hesitate to ask for help when your child needs it.

When Brennan was eight, he wrote me a note saying that life was hard and he didn't like living. I was having so much trouble knowing how to handle him and his feelings that I sought a therapist's help. The professional assistance we received made a very positive impact on Brennan and my ability to parent him.

I highly recommend seeking help for psychological problems, in the same way we seek help for physical problems. A professional therapist can provide a sounding board that is distinctly different from all others by creating a nonjudgmental, safe place in which to examine the problems. For some of us, there is still a stigma attached to psychological assistance. Try not to let that stand in the way of asking for the best possible help for your child. The best source of recommendations is your doctor or nurse-educator or another parent who has sought counseling. You don't have to see a psychiatrist unless a severe depression is noted. A licensed psychologist or family counselor can offer valuable insight and be much less expensive. If possible, try to find a therapist who knows something about diabetes or at the very least works with children with chronic illnesses.

One parent asked me if a therapist could get his teenager to stick to his diet. It is certainly a parent's and doctor's fantasy that a therapist will make a child comply, but compliance, per se, is not the role of the therapist. If the therapist lectures and takes the stance of another authority figure who tries to control, she will lose the ear of her client. The goal of the therapist is to provide a time for the child to talk about what's on his mind and help reduce stress. Compliance may follow, but of the child's own volition.

The purpose of therapy is to open up the lines of communication. Studies and professional observation have shown that children from families with good communication skills are more likely to have their diabetes in good control.

YOUR CHILD'S FEELINGS

We've looked at how you can help your child express his feelings; now let's examine some of the underlying emotional issues and their possible manifestations. These include denial and/or acceptance of diabetes, isolation, fear, anger, and rebellion.

Denial/Acceptance

Your child's acceptance of his diabetes will begin with your own acceptance. Young children believe that their parents are all-powerful and diabetic children sometimes think that their parents can take the diabetes away. It's important for your child to know that he and you must accept what has happened, that nothing either of you did caused it, and there's nothing you can do to take it away.

A small child cannot make logical sense of detailed explanations, so you don't have to have all the answers. A matter-of-fact approach, a tone of confidence, and a spirit of "we'll get through this together" works best. Keep your explanation as simple and as concrete as possible and expressed in terms your child can understand.

When Brennan was four, we explained it with this example: "You know that Mommy and Daddy wear glasses when we read or watch television. That's because our eyes don't work too well. You have a special part of your body called a pancreas which also doesn't work too well. You need to take shots of insulin so that you can feel good."

After an initial explanation, you can answer specific questions as they arise. One of the toughest for me was, "When will my shots be over?" I couldn't bring myself to say "never," so I said "I don't know." (Even though I was telling the truth, I felt I was hedging. However, since I now believe that research will find a cure, I realize "I don't know" was not such a bad answer after all.)

Small children will follow their parents' lead in accepting diabetes rather quickly, but a school-aged child will also be influenced by his peers. He may not want others to know that he has diabetes. I recall a letter from a mother who was very worried because her daughter didn't want anyone to know about her diabetes. She thought that her daughter's wish for complete privacy was actually a form of denial.

When I asked pediatric endocrinologist Dr. Robert Clemons how this mother should handle the situation, he responded that the daughter shouldn't have to tell everyone if she didn't wish to do so. If she was taking her shots and blood tests and being responsible about her diet, she was obviously acknowledging and not denying that she had diabetes and was merely being private about it.

At the same time, he recommended that she be encouraged to let some people who were close to her know. Perhaps she felt that diabetes was something to be ashamed of. If so, this girl needed help in seeing the other side: that good friends would respect her ability to deal with all the shots and finger pricks. Once she understood this, she might need to practice how to tell her friends. It's scary to tell people something important about ourselves when we feel they might reject us.

However, there could be more here than meets the eye. This young girl was twelve years old, old enough to understand the impact that diabetes was having on her life. She might have just become aware of what the future could hold with regard to complications. She might have been experiencing a sense of loss, a fear of the future, might even have been somewhat depressed. The early adolescent is very concerned with body image. The distinction of having diabetes can be very distressing for some children.

If a child's refusal to talk about diabetes is accompanied by falling grades, weight loss, or other big changes in outward behavior, she might need extra help. If she refuses to open up and talk with a parent or other adult, her parents should ask the doctor to recommend a therapist to help this girl explore her feelings.

Isolation

The issue of isolation is a painful one for children because they want to belong and be part of the group. Belonging and "being part of" helps them define who they are. Anything that separates or makes them different can bring on responses that range from frustration to depression.

How your child's diabetes is handled in the school setting will have a powerful effect on your child's feelings about himself. It is your child's decision to tell his classmates that he has diabetes. Yet, it is a good idea for a few of his close friends to know the signs of an insulin reaction and how to help. Also, the parents of these close friends should know, especially if your child will be spending time at their homes. Discuss with your child the need for letting some of these people know.

Of course, all of your child's teachers and responsible adults at school should know about your child's diabetes and be willing and able to treat an insulin reaction. Both JDF and ADA have pamphlets that explain diabetes to school personnel.

That doesn't necessarily mean all will go smoothly. One little girl was doing some angry acting-out at school that baffled her mother. A little detective work uncovered the cause—her daughter was being taken from class for her snack at 10:30 instead of being allowed to have her snack during the normal break time of 10:40. The mother had told them she needed a snack around 10:30 and they took her request quite literally. Her daughter was feeling embarrassed and isolated from her classmates. Once her mother assured the teacher that her daughter could eat her snack at 10:40, everything smoothed out.

When Brennan was in third grade, his teacher would excuse him to have his midmorning snack. One of the other boys asked Brennan why he could leave class to eat. Brennan said he had to eat because he had diabetes. The boy's response was, "Ooh, get away from me. You have a disease." Brennan's reaction was very subdued. He didn't have much to say about it, although I could tell he was hurt by the comments. We talked about the fact that the boy's cruelty was based on his ignorance of diabetes. I had always been very forthright about telling people that Brennan had diabetes. After that incident, I decided I would never mention Brennan's diabetes to any of his friends unless he gave me permission.

Recently I received a letter from a mother who wrote, "Realize that your child wants to be treated as normal. Don't direct unnecessary attention toward his diabetes. For example, instead of ordering the diabetic meal on the airline, I should just have had the regular meal served. It was not that much different and the attention focused on Matt caused him much distress."

Of course, some children have no problem letting others know. One little girl brought her blood testing equipment to school for show-and-tell. Another boy presented a science report about diabetes which caused a classmate to remark, "I had diarrhea once, too."

One young girl used her artistic talents to share her diabetes with her class. She told her mother that she'd easily recognize which drawing of the body was hers at the next open house. Her mother was surprised to find an "out-of-order" sign where the pancreas should have been.

Most of your child's peer group will be impressed with his bravery once they understand that having diabetes means daily shots and blood tests. Some, however, can be obnoxious. Teach your child to be assertive. He might say something such as, "My body has trouble with the way it handles sugar. I have to watch what I eat, test my blood several times, and give myself shots every day. Could you do that?"

For a teenager, the pressure to be part of the gang is stronger than ever. Spontaneity and unpredictable behavior are the hallmark of being with teenaged friends. Diabetes asks a teen to limit much of that spontaneity by calculating and planning even the most basic activities. Deciding to have a pizza after a football game with the gang is a normal activity for a teen, but for your teenager it can mean a very high blood sugar. So now he has a choice to make: take care of his diabetes or go along with the gang. He may go along with the group, but feel anxious and guilty because he hasn't done what he knows is right regarding his diabetes. Yet, being the same as the others and fitting in are of prime importance to him, and not being able to have pizza make him feel angry or, at the very least, constrained.

Planning ahead can help avoid the feelings of anger or guilt. A teen who is on a three-shot program has more flexibility than one who is on only two shots. In the case of the pizza, he could determine how many pieces of pizza he wants and, using the carbohydrate to be eaten as a guide to insulin dosage, inject himself in private in the bathroom. Of course, that means sitting down with his dietitian and physician ahead of time and knowing the formula to use for adjusting the insulin dose.

Support groups and summer camps offer opportunities for your child to overcome any isolation he might feel and to experience an increased sense of control. One young girl, Christi, was diagnosed at age eight. For the first ten months, she was completely dependent on her parents for all her care. Then she went to diabetes summer camp. When her parents picked her up two weeks later she had taken complete charge of her shots and blood tests. The ADA can provide information regarding camps in your area.

Knowing that you're not alone helps. When Brennan was twelve, he made friends with another boy who had diabetes. I took them out to dinner and since they were sitting across the table from me, Adam offered to help Brennan with his shot. Brennan said, "It's nice to have a friend with diabetes." It certainly is. Meeting other young people with diabetes can be very helpful. Check with the ADA to see what youth support groups exist in your area.

Another wonderful source of support is available at Children's Hospital in Los Angeles. It's a mentor program that matches diabetic adolescents with adult sponsors who also have diabetes. The adults provide good role models because they are successful in their professions and have their diabetes in good control. The sponsors and adolescents who have participated have been enthusiastic about the results of their relationships. Many of the young people felt less secretive about their diabetes and more confident about themselves. Their comments illustrate the success of the program:

"I had bad habits, and he really helped me understand what I needed to do."

"I never used to carry my supplies or tell people, and that has changed. I liked to be with someone where it didn't get in the way, and maybe I can carry that into the real world."

"He taught me that I am still normal and that I can do anything."

"I'm more secure with my diabetes by knowing someone who had made it."

This was a pilot program, a study whose results can be obtained by writing Beverly Daley, Ph.D., c/o Children's Hospital Los Angeles, 4650 Sunset Blvd., Box 38, Los Angeles 90027.

Fear

There are fears that may arise as a result of having diabetes: fear of injections, fear that other diseases may occur, fear of insulin reactions. Listen carefully to what your child says or how he acts, and use active listening or "wonder if" to help him articulate his fears. Allow your child to freely express whatever frightens him. Try not to judge or dismiss his fears. For young children, drawing or playing with dolls or puppets will help alleviate some of the scariness.

Don't worry about not being able to completely eradicate your child's fears. Let him know that it's all right to be afraid and what matters is doing what we have to do in spite of our fears. Support and acknowledge the courage he shows by talking about what frightens him. One mother whose daughter is afraid of having shots puts a gold star on a chart on the refrigerator every time she is cooperative in spite of her fears.

Since the world of the younger child is very now oriented, these children don't really comprehend the long-term consequences of diabetes. Actually, it is not appropriate to discuss complications with your child until he is in his teens. Such a discussion will not be fully comprehensible to a younger child and may only serve to frighten him.

Yet, even if you don't directly mention complications, your child may hear of them from other people. Someone might say, "Diabetes—it's awful. My aunt died of diabetes." Or "My grandfather went blind because of diabetes."

If your child brings up the subject, get an understanding of his knowledge of the complications first. Your discussion should convey both concern, because complications can happen, and optimism, since the prognosis for children with diabetes is getting better all the time. Keep your explanation as general and nonthreatening as possible. Something such as, "Diabetes can hurt some people if they don't take good care of themselves" is best. Give honest, straightforward answers to your child's questions. If a child senses that you're hiding something, his imaginary fears may be much worse than reality. Be sure to stress the immediate rewards of controlling diabetes such as feeling good, growing well, and having more energy for school and sports.

It is very important that you never use scare tactics to encourage better health habits. Diabetes can be scary enough as it is. (Sometimes, scare tactics can backfire in the teen years, leading to reckless behavior because "What the hell, I'm going to die anyway.")

What if your child mentions that he is concerned that he might die? It is certainly a disturbing question to hear from a child with diabetes.

There are several elements to consider in formulating an answer. One is the age of your child. Up to the age of six, the primary fear is one of separation. From six to eleven, pain and death are of great concern. First of all, listen to the way your child phrases the question. If he's worried that diabetes may cause his death, you need to tell the truth in a very nonthreatening, positive way. For example, "Diabetes is a disease that some people can die from, especially if they've had it a very long time, but you're doing very well. That's why it's so important that you take good care of yourself."

Try to understand what your child's needs are at that moment. If he's merely asking a general question about death, don't inject your own fears into the conversation or answer what you're afraid he *might* be asking. If you're not sure what he wants to know, ask him to be more specific. Then answer the exact question your child asks. Don't go into a detailed description if it's not needed. Build a base of information and expand it as he gets older and the questions get more detailed.

Anger

There are so many demands made of a child who has diabetes. They can make your child feel very angry at times.

Five-year-old Justin was being coaxed to eat more dinner. His father said, "Come on, be a good boy." Suddenly, all the pent-up frustration and anger, the pressure of daily blood tests and shots, the rude awakenings at midnight for snacks to head off insulin reactions came to a boil. Justin screamed, "I'm always a good boy! I'm tired of being good!"

He stormed off to his room in tears. His father went to him and as he held him said, "I know it's hard having diabetes. Mommy and I would have diabetes in a minute if it meant you would get better." The anger subsided and he looked up at his father. Quietly he said, "No one should have diabetes."

Children need to learn how to deal with anger and frustration. Use active listening and the other previously listed techniques to let your child know that there are acceptable ways to express his anger.

At some time or other, your diabetic child may resent that he has diabetes and his sibling doesn't. Listening without judging can assist him in handling these feelings. Sometimes, the feelings will manifest as undesirable behavior. Letting your child know that the behavior is not acceptable can be balanced by listening and reflecting his feelings in a nonjudgmental way. "I cannot allow you to hit your brother. I know you're feeling angry and I don't blame you. If I had diabetes, I would feel angry sometimes, too. It's okay to be angry. It is not okay for you to take your anger out on your brother."

I'll never forget one night at a JDF fund-raiser. I was conducting an auction and people were being very generous. Suddenly, I felt a tug on my jacket. I looked down into the eight-year-old face of my son, Robin. He handed me $5.00 and said, "I saved this from my allowance." He stood at my side until the auction was through. Then I took him up into my arms and praised his unselfish donation. With tears in his eyes, he said, "It was my only $5.00. I gave it to help diabetes. You know, Brennan's diabetes is hard on me, too."

"Oh, honey," I said. "Is it hard on you?"

"Yeah. Brennan gets mad and beats me up."

Robin's story might have made me smile, but it saddened me, too. Needless to say, I talked to Brennan and tried to help him not make Robin suffer for Brennan's diabetes.

Sometimes anger can come from unexpected places. Lisa, the little girl whose story I told in chapter 2, spent so much time in the hospital that she was angry when she came home because she was no longer the center of attention. At the same time, she was angry at her mom and dad for sending her away to the hospital. When she got home, she threw tantrums.

Her mother told me, "She missed the constant attention of the hospital personnel catering to her desires. She also didn't understand why she was being hurt when she hadn't done anything wrong. We gave her lots of hugs, told her repeatedly we loved her, and that we would rather she slept at home with us. After her fourth visit, she finally accepted the purpose of her admits (hospitalizations)."

Sometimes, the stress of feeling angry can cause high blood sugars. One teenaged girl had a blood sugar test over 300 until she reconciled with her girlfriend after an argument. Times of family stress and crises can also powerfully affect blood sugar levels. At such times, exercise and counseling can help to reduce stress and lead toward more controlled blood sugars.

Living with diabetes, knowing it will always be there, is not easy. There will be anger, there will be tears. There will be "It's not fair." Once again, allowing anger its rightful time and respecting your child's feelings will help more than trying to suppress or deflect the anger. When the anger is spent, move your child's attention toward the positive elements of his life— all he can do, all he does have. If the anger has grown out of his comparing himself to someone who does not have diabetes, identify and praise the positive differences.

Work to assist your child to have a strong image of himself so that he sees himself as a child who has diabetes, not a diabetic child. As one mother lovingly describes her son, "Matthew is a child first. The diabetes is only one aspect of the total being that encompasses his mind and body. He is an artist, a runner, a mimic, a dancer, a joyful blond child, and a crabby blond child, a host of things."

Rebellion

Rebellion in its greater or lesser forms is a natural part of growing up. Your child's rebelliousness will depend on myriad influences, not the least of which is his individual temperament. The problem with a rebellious child with diabetes is, of course, that his lack of cooperation may undermine his health. With younger children, charm, cleverness, and a sense of humor will usually solve most problems. After all, they can't do very much without your supervision or approval.

These young ones will, however, test your inventiveness and patience. A child who is diagnosed under five years old, at the initial stages of independence, could wind up fighting you about any or all of the new rules imposed on him.

Inherent in a toddler's quest for independence is a certain amount of rebellion. Unfortunately, power struggles will sometimes center around food. Try not to get into battles over food. If your child won't eat one thing, try another. Finger foods, juice, frozen yogurt bars, or decorated foods may be appealing. There's nothing wrong with cereal for dinner. You can be flexible without feeling you're doing a song and dance. Try not to give extra attention if your child is not eating.

Sometimes, nothing you do works. Rather than try to force-feed a fussy eater, wait and let the natural consequences occur. One of two things will happen: the lower blood sugar will cause your child to feel hungry (problem solved!) or he may begin to experience an insulin reaction. If you're watchful and prepared with a sugar source—juice, glucose, gel, soft drink, or milk—you'll catch it quickly. After the reaction has subsided, you can talk to your child about why it happened and how he'll feel better if he eats his snacks and meals on time. Sooner or later, your child will understand that not eating makes him feel bad. You don't need to scold or punish. It only reinforces negative behavior. Work on positive reinforcement. You might suggest a book you're going to read together as soon as the snack or meal is eaten or sit down and eat with your child.

One diabetic four-year-old thought he had figured out how to stay up later. He made his snack of popcorn last for over an hour. When his mom said, "Finish up or you'll go to bed without your snack," he replied, "No, Mommy, I'm diabetic!"

Dealing with a diabetic toddler is a challenge. See if you can locate another parent like yourself in your community to help get you through the tough times. Even though it's not written specifically about toddlers who have diabetes, I suggest reading the book *Disciplining Your Preschooler and Feeling Good About It* by Mitch and Susan Golant, listed in the Resources section. It has good, basic advice for parents about setting limits, establishing discipline, and understanding age-appropriate behavior.

Another issue that masquerades as rebellion is departure from the diet plan. Time for a parental "reality check." You can't really expect anyone, much less a child, to always stick to a preplanned diet. When departures occur, be as nonjudgmental as possible. "You had a candy bar. I'm glad you told me. Now we know what caused this high blood sugar. Let's talk to your doctor to see how to bring it back to normal." You can discuss what your child can do the next time he has an urge to eat something not included in his diet plan. Emphasize the "can haves," not the "can't haves."

Your dietitian or nurse-educator can help you figure acceptable treats into the insulin dosage or just before a period of exercise. Remember, one of anything is not going to irreparably harm your child. The emphasis should be on a basic consistency and keeping the lines of communication open. You don't want your child to tune you out because he's heard the same old harangue too many times.

You may notice I do not use the word "cheating." Paul Madden of the Joslin Diabetes Center in Boston recommends that we drop the word "cheating" from our diabetes vocabulary. It conveys a judgmental, moralistic tone that is not supportive or helpful. Try substituting the word "overeating" or using the phrase "you ate more than your body needed at the time."

The task of coping with rebellion becomes much harder after your dear one reaches thirteen or so. One mother swears that her daughter lost her mind on her thirteenth birthday and reappeared as a rational human being shortly after her seventeenth. She had always been a sweet, extremely agreeable child. The morning she turned thirteen, her mother greeted her with a loving "Good morning. Happy birthday, sweetheart!" Her daughter burst into tears and ran sobbing from the room. "I couldn't do or say a thing to please her for four years." Now the mother can laugh about it, but the rejection and confusion that she felt at the time were very hard for her.

The teen years span a turbulent period of becoming an individual, separate but equal (or so they think!) to one's parents. Defining "Who am I?" is a primary task of these years. Part of that individuation is a rejection of much of what the parents appear to be. Teens can be very critical of their parents. Many times, they are absolutely sure they are right and that their parents can't possibly understand them.

There are so many conflicted feelings for a teen. He is a child and wants to be taken care of. He is an adult and wants to make all his own decisions. One father I know has a sign on his refrigerator which reads, "Teenagers! Are you tired of being pushed around by teachers and parents? Fight back! Move out now, while you still know everything!"

It is very difficult to be a teen who has diabetes. Diabetes is, quite simply, not what being a teenager is all about. One teenaged boy who refused to keep his diabetes in control said succinctly, "Diabetes doesn't fit into my lifestyle."

Adolescents are obsessed with controlling their own lives and defining their identities. This involves a great deal of experimentation and rebellion. It is a difficult time for parents as it is. Add diabetes and it can feel overwhelmingly impossible at times.

Independence is the issue. Up until this time, you may have been able to dictate what your child did and what he ate, but no more. As he sees it, it's his life, not yours, and he's going to find out how he wants to live. Even though teens have the ability to understand long-term complications, some teens may not take them seriously or don't think about them much, while others are overwhelmed by the threat of problems later on. Nagging and threats just don't work. Keeping communication open is vital.

Your teenager is taking over management of his diabetes just at the time when, for physiological reasons, his blood sugar is becoming harder to control. Teenagers can actually develop a physical resistance to insulin due to increased hormonal activity. So they usually take larger doses than adults of the same weight. Also, the mechanism that protects the body from low blood sugars works a little harder in a teenager, causing blood sugars to frequently bounce back up. Control can be even more difficult for teenaged girls because their menstrual cycle, with its attendant estrogen and progesterone, alters insulin needs. It appears that rising hormonal levels reduce insulin effectiveness.

It would be ideal to have the diabetic teen stick to his diet all the time, but who's ideal? Machines maybe, but not teenagers. One option is to demand rigid compliance and say, "This is what you're supposed to do, now do it." Or, to quote Dr. Raymonde Herkowitz, a pediatric endocrinologist at the Joslin Diabetes Center, "You can help them learn to make choices, and teach them the measured freedom that comes from planning."

Even if your teen is trying to be cooperative, planning ahead can be difficult because of all the last-minute changes that can happen. It becomes important to plan for the unexpected, too. That means your teen needs to keep some source of sugar and food nearby at all times. If he's on a sports team, that means cans of juice and other snacks in his sports bag and his locker, plus keeping a little money in his pocket in case he needs to stop and get some food to fend off a low blood sugar. Also, keeping some blood testing equipment handy at all times can help him make better choices.

A teen with poorly controlled blood sugar may have reactions in front of his friends, which can be embarrassing. An episode or two of that and a teen may have a new reason to take better care of himself. In spite of this, a teenager may test the limits of not paying attention to his diabetes. After all, testing limits is what being a teen is all about.

For some teens, these years are more difficult than for others. Whatever the degree of compliance, there is not much you can do about it directly. You cannot stand over your teen's shoulder and monitor what he does every minute. You cannot stop him from doing something self-destructive. It's part of the essential powerlessness of being a parent. Knowing that doesn't make it any easier, but at least you can be realistic.

For a moment, put yourself in his shoes. He has a disease which, at this point in time, is permanent and requires daily and hourly care and concern. He faces the constant struggle between satisfying his immediate desires and knowing his long-term health may be at stake. That's a struggle for anyone, much less someone who is going through the disruptive forces of the teenage years.

Food becomes more of a problem for teens. They don't want to stick to a diet. Rebellion can take the form of abandoning the established diabetes regimen, overeating, and eating supposedly forbidden foods. To avoid dealing with parental reminders (also known as nagging!), the less-than-desirable foods are often eaten in secret. As a parent, it's difficult to adjust an insulin dose when you don't know what your child is eating.

Foods labeled as "never" are more enticing, so it's a good idea to have as few "never" foods as possible. Of course, it takes planning, in conjunction with an active lifestyle, to make that work. It also takes an understanding dietitian who has some sense of the teenage mindset, one who is willing to teach all the ways to deal with excursions from the approved diet. Some parents have a tough time accepting that it's okay for their teens to be eating ice cream and potato chips occasionally. Yet it is good for your teen to know that there are ways to overeat that minimize the negative effects on blood sugar control. They're probably going to do it anyway, so we might as well give them all the knowledge they need to care for their diabetes effectively.

Hopefully, you have a good diabetes team who can help you not be the bad guy too much of the time. By forming a strong relationship with your teen, these professionals can support good diabetes management and leave you to deal more with other issues such as school, curfews, and car keys. Being clear in your mind about priorities is vital. I remember when Brennan decided that he had to pierce his ear and then, later, to lighten his hair. He said, "Mom, I'm a teenager now and I want to experiment with how I look and what I wear." I agreed that it was *his* hair and he could do whatever he wanted with it. I told him that as long as he worked hard in school and took care of his diabetes, he could dye his hair magenta, if he liked. (God forbid!)

Leave your teen room to rebel. Loud music, crazy clothes and hairdos, and weird makeup are part of these years. As I see it, the only things worth fighting for during these years are the issues that may damage your child's future—drugs, drinking, unsafe driving, bad grades, and not controlling his diabetes. Everything else will pass.

It is his disease, after all, and the sooner you allow him to "own" it, the better. I'm not suggesting that you wash your hands of it, because that is impossible. There is much you can do to guide and support positive behavior. Give him as much knowledge as possible while continuing to supervise and provide positive reinforcement. Consider yourself as a consultant. Discuss the choices together and let your teen decide what to do. If you disagree with his choice, let him know what choice you think is better and why, then leave it at that. See if your teen can describe how he sees your role in his diabetes care. Let him know how you view your role and negotiate the differences.

Also, check with your local ADA and JDF chapters to see what teen support groups might be available in your area.

SPECIAL PROBLEMS FOR TEENS

There are two problem areas that affect and are affected by emotional and psychological elements of a teen's personality. Each presents a specific threat to a diabetic teen's well-being. One is eating disorders; the other is the consumption of alcohol or drugs.

Eating Disorders

The eating disorders anorexia nervosa and bulimia nervosa are characterized by a preoccupation with food, body shape, and weight. Teenaged girls are more likely than boys to develop eating disorders that can be extremely dangerous. Anorexia involves severe weight loss to the point where a girl stops menstruating, develops a distorted body image, and has a fear of gaining weight and becoming fat. Bulimia involves patterns of binge eating, followed by self-induced vomiting or other methods of preventing weight gain.

The teen with diabetes is at special risk because her metabolic system is already not working properly. Even an occasional binge can affect control, contributing to unstable blood sugars, frequent hypoglycemia, ketoacidosis, and hospitalization. Diabetes is a powerful tool for purging. If a teen with diabetes doesn't take enough insulin, her body can't use the food it's eaten. The excess calories spill into the urine and she loses weight just as she did when first diagnosed. She can literally waste away.

A diabetic teen who wants to lose weight should do so under the careful guidance of a professional. It is very hard to diet while taking insulin. Girls who take insulin tend to lay down more fat than those who don't. The better the blood sugar control the more likely a weight gain. The gain is usually minor, maybe five pounds, but to a girl overly concerned with body image, this can feel like a disaster.

For a teen who doesn't have an eating disorder but who is concerned about weight, regular exercise can be the key to controlled blood sugars and maintaining a good figure. Find an activity that is fun and is done on a regular basis—any team sport, tennis, gymnastics, swimming, dancing, cheerleading, or aerobic exercise, for example.

Many factors—biological, and psychological, as well as pressure from family and friends—contribute to the development of an eating disorder. If your teen is losing a noticeable amount of weight on her own, check with your doctor about the possibility of an eating disorder. Don't let it go unattended; it is not something that will just "go away," and you'll need professional help in dealing with it.

Alcohol and Drugs

There is so much awareness regarding drugs and alcohol these days. They are a danger to all our children, but even more so for young people with diabetes. Anything that alters your child's senses places him more at risk.

Alcohol affects a person with diabetes in interesting ways. While it makes the drinker feel high, it actually lowers blood sugar and impairs judgment. A diabetic teen is more likely to have a serious reaction while drinking, and the people around him may think he is only drunk and leave him alone.

Alcohol is a rich source of calories with almost no nutritional value. While the liver is busy processing the alcohol, it is prevented from releasing stored sugar to counteract a reaction. Thus, the danger to a diabetic is twofold. Sometimes people who are drinking forget to eat, which for your teen would likely lead to a reaction, and, with the liver unable to release glucose, the reaction can be even more severe than otherwise.

Let your teen know that if he does have a drink on occasion, he should do so only when he has already eaten and his diabetes is in good control. Even a glass of milk can help protect the stomach and the brain. Your child needs to understand that if he has a severe reaction while drinking, people will think he's drunk and not offer assistance. An unattended reaction can be dangerous and cause brain damage. Someone with him should know he has diabetes and know how to treat an insulin reaction. He should wear a Medic Alert bracelet or medallion at all times.

Your teen should not drive if he's had even one drink because of the increased possibility of a reaction. Discuss in advance how he might feel pressure at a party to drink to be a part of the gang. One solution is to offer himself as the DD, the designated driver, when he goes out with his friends.

You also have the opportunity to set an example by the manner in which you use alcohol. Use it sparingly and respectfully, if at all. It will be difficult to get your teen to abstain if you drink frequently and to excess.

Drugs are illegal. Period. Under no circumstances should your teen be using them. If either drugs or alcohol become a problem for him, let his doctor know immediately. Then I suggest contacting Alcoholics Anonymous for help. They have groups for drug-related problems, as well as for alcohol.

I suppose it's hard to imagine that a teen who has to use a syringe for insulin every day may decide to shoot up with something else, too. Yet, the syringes can create problems separate from how they are used.

Brennan attended a party not too long ago and went to the bathroom just before dinner to take his shot. Two weeks later, I received a call from the woman who had given the party. After several minutes of her testing the waters, she asked me if I was aware that my son was using drugs. She had found a syringe in the wastebasket in her bathroom and, though her son had told her that Brennan was diabetic, she decided it was probably just a cover story. She had called many people, including my son's school, to inform them of her discovery.

I was less than thrilled that she had been so indiscreet. After assuring her that, "Yes, Brennan does have diabetes," I had a long talk with my son. We agreed that it was best to always bring his used syringes home and discard them to avoid misunderstandings like that again.

In helping our children grow and learn to cope with their lives, we have the opportunity to continue to grow and learn about ourselves. As we allow them a safe place to experience their feelings, we can also create a harbor for our own hearts. If perhaps we were not listened to as children, we now have the chance, by extending ourselves to our children out of love, to parent them and also to "reparent" ourselves. And that leads us to the next chapter.

6

What About Me?

Not too long ago, I was in Nashville for a fund-raising dinner for the Juvenile Diabetes Foundation International. At the reception afterward, a woman introduced herself and began to tell me about her daughter's recent diagnosis. The sadness and anger that filled her face and voice transported me back to those first months after Brennan's diagnosis. I understood what she was feeling as only another parent could.

I have been there. I know what you are feeling, what you have felt. You and I have known a most terrible letting go. We have been forced to let go of the myth that we can protect our children. In her essential book, *Necessary Losses,* Judith Viorst empathizes with our dream of keeping our little ones safe from every harm. In the chapter titled "Saving the Children," she writes, "We will have to let go of so much of what we hoped we could do for our children." I cried all the way through that section.

No, we cannot "fix" our children's diabetes, but we know that the way we handle this challenge makes an enormous difference to our children. Up until now, this book has provided information and techniques that assist you in helping your child live successfully with diabetes. Now we investigate what we as parents can do to take care of ourselves and live up to the many emotional and psychological demands that diabetes has brought into our lives. We will cover your feelings and what to do about them. We'll also examine how to help other members of your family handle their feelings, how to motivate them to assist in caring for your child and his diabetes, and how to educate others with whom your child will have contact. We will discuss the importance of becoming an advocate for your child and spell out the steps you can take to ensure that your child's school provides support for his diabetes needs.

TEABAGS ALL

You know the truth, intellectually at least, that life is difficult. That nobody promised you a rose garden. That nobody said it was going to be easy. All those little homilies that are supposed to make it hurt less. They don't. Your child's diabetes still feels like a death.

And it is. It is the death of the expectation that your child will grow up unencumbered, that there is no limit to his life. Like any loss, it must be accompanied by a time for grieving. Grief is not only sadness, it can also encompass anger, guilt, denial, confusion, and anxiety. When we have allowed ourselves time and ways of working through these feelings, we come through to the other side: acceptance.

Of course, some of us get through it more quickly than others. One mother wrote me that eight months after her daughter's diagnosis, she still found it difficult to get through even one day without crying. She felt her depression would never end. At the same time, her daughter was doing very well.

Every parent I have ever met whose child has had diabetes for a long time has been amazed at how lost they felt in the beginning, and yet how much they learned and how well they did. To quote writer Rita Mae Brown,

"People are like teabags; you don't know how strong they'll be until they're in hot water." So here we are, teabags all: parents who are learning the depth of their feelings for their children and discovering strengths they didn't know they had.

In dealing with all these feelings that our children's diabetes breeds, it helps to understand the expectations we hold. We all have expectations, both conscious and unconscious. Some are met and surpassed, some never realized. One mother told me that she was angry at the unfairness, because she was feeling so out of control. Had she really expected to be able to control and handle everything that happened to her child? Perhaps, deep in her heart, that expectation had been planted. Now she had to face its undoing. So goes the rest of our lives. As we grow, we need to adjust our expectations to include the reality we encounter.

I have a dear friend named Wendy with whom I deeply shared my first years of motherhood. We both have two boys who were born within the same two-year span. We spoke once about our dreams for our children. "Remember," I said, "when the first one was born, we were going to teach him about God and the trees and the flowers and he was going to be the most special child anyone had ever seen? And then with the second one, you didn't care about his being special, you just wanted him to be normal?"

"Special?" Wendy replied. "I just don't want him to grow up to be an ax killer!"

Yes, our expectations do change. We expect that our children will act a certain way; they do not. We don't expect that they will have a chronic illness; they do. We expect ourselves to be much better parents than our parents were. Most likely, we are not. Even more likely, we find ourselves doing exactly what our parents did. There is a good reason for this.

Parenting involves reliving your own childhood. It is inevitable that you will replay events of your own childhood with your children. You will basically treat your children the way you were treated. It is the only reference you have and you have thoroughly incorporated it into your behavior. What you learned in childhood, by way of example, is what you expect a child-parent relationship to encompass.

I believe that parenting is the most difficult job we take on in our lives. In order to be good parents we must be willing to constantly reassess ourselves and our actions. We have inherited a certain way of parenting and learned a certain way of working in the world. It is very difficult to uproot those old behaviors and fashion a new way of living. Some of us have the added burden of feeling we have to be perfect and be all things to all people. Be gentle with yourself; you are just as much a "work in progress" as your child.

We learn, if we are open to it, just as much from our children as they learn from us. Diabetes intensifies that learning process, forcing us to extend ourselves beyond what we envisioned as our capabilities. We face the saddest of possibilities: the mortality of our children. We become more aware of the fragility of life. As one mother wrote me, "I don't take life for granted. When I do, Craig [her diabetic son] reminds me just by being here."

FEELINGS, NOTHING MORE THAN FEELINGS

The diagnosis of your child's diabetes has brought a crisis into your life. There are many intense feelings that surface because of this crisis. They demand your acknowledgment. Feelings don't go away just because you ignore them. Talking about them, writing about them, bringing them out into the open to let a little light shine on them takes away some of their power. Feelings are sources of energy that can be focused in positive or negative directions. That energy can be used to learn and grow, or it can be poured into inappropriately directed anger and depression.

You may feel that it is necessary to keep a stiff upper lip and carry on, hiding your feelings from almost everyone around you. It's fine to be the strong one, but sooner or later you need to deal with the emotions that you feel. To quote Mr. Shakespeare:

Give sorrow words; the grief that does not speak

Whispers the oe'r fraught heart, and bids it break.

Let's give sorrow words and look at some of the feelings you may have experienced since your child's diagnosis: anger, guilt, denial/acceptance, and confusion.

Anger

When you are first told about your child's diabetes, you want to make sense of it. There must be someone to blame, right? You might find anger flaring up. You might feel angry with your doctor, your spouse, yourself, even your child. Anger is perfectly understandable. You're angry at the diabetes, not at those you love and respect. It's difficult, though, to direct anger at something as abstract as a disease.

Talking about the anger will help you see it for what it is. Anger is often the way we react to hurt and fear and loss. Your anger and frustration might also stem from your feeling that you're not getting enough support. You need to let those around you know that and negotiate their assistance.

Guilt

Diabetes might have existed on your side of the family. Perhaps you feel guilty for "giving" your child diabetes. Of course, you didn't give him diabetes. Giving is an act of purpose and you did not purposely give your child diabetes.

I remember feeling guilty because a doctor doing a survey told me that babies over 9 pounds had an increased chance of getting diabetes. Brennan's birth weight was 9 pounds, 1 ounce and I started to feel bad that I'd had a big baby; as if I'd had control over exactly what he weighed. I sat myself down and talked myself out of that one real fast!

Many parents have guilt feelings because of the pain and discomfort from shots and finger pricks they give to their children. It is so terribly difficult to hold your child down and to have him fight and cry as you give the shot or blood test. You must keep reminding yourself that you are doing it out of love as well as trying to protect your child's life and health.

You might think that you didn't feed your child the right foods and somehow contributed to the onset of the diabetes. Yet, as you become educated about diabetes, you learn that nothing you did or didn't do caused your child to have diabetes. (If you still have any doubts about that issue, they will be cleared up after reading chapter 7.)

You may want to beat yourself up for not recognizing the symptoms sooner. Go easy. You did the best you could. There are doctors who have not recognized diabetes when all the symptoms were staring right at them.

You might find yourself feeling guilty if your child has a reaction. I heard from one mom who told me about the time her daughter, Jill, and her friend, Stacy, were playing on opposing softball teams. Both girls have diabetes. The two moms were sitting in the stands, swapping diabetes coping methods, when both girls walked off the field, complaining of not feeling well. Blood tests were done; glucose tablets and snacks were consumed. No harm done, right? Yet, Jill's mom felt the need to apologize. She felt guilty because she hadn't been paying close attention. Jill looked at her and said, "Mom, it was great. I never had a reaction with anyone before!"

That mother's guilt was based on her expectation that she should have known and done something about an insulin reaction ahead of time, even though there was no possible way for her to have done that. Clearly, this is unrealistic.

To my way of thinking, guilt is a useless feeling. It doesn't necessarily lead to positive action; it only makes us feel bad about ourselves. It's much more productive to take a guilt-free inventory of a situation. Look at what happened without punishing yourself and see what you might have done better or what you might learn from your mistakes. Feel free to talk back to guilt whenever it rears its ugly head.

Denial/Acceptance

You may go through a period of denial. You wake up in the morning and feel that perhaps your child's diabetes is all a bad dream. Then the reality hits and you find yourself feeling the weight of the diagnosis all over again. Something in your mind doesn't want to let the truth sink in.

Eventually, you do accept that diabetes is here to stay. This acceptance grows out of living with diabetes for a while and from explaining to others over and over that, no, your child will not "grow out of it." I remember how angry I felt when people told me that my son's diabetes would go away as he grew older. I know now that I wasn't angry at them so much as I was angry at the "all his life" part of Brennan's diabetes. I didn't want to be constantly reminded that there was no end in sight.

In a sense, you're not really denying that your child has diabetes because real denial would mean an unwillingness on your part to acknowledge that your child has diabetes. If that were the case, you would not be reading this book! You may be at the stage where you're still trying to push diabetes away. You're just not ready to really accept it as a permanent fixture.

The secret, as bizarre as it might sound, is to fully embrace diabetes and take it on as a personal responsibility. That which we deny, that which we run from, has power over us. We regain a sense of control by including diabetes as an accepted part of our world. You can use any one or several of the techniques discussed in this chapter to come to acceptance. Picture and affirm that your life now includes diabetes and that it is a good life, filled with great love and intensity. See diabetes as part of your life that serves a positive purpose. Perhaps, like me, through getting involved in diabetes research and becoming an advocate, your life will gain a momentum and a richness it never had before. Perhaps you will find yourself growing, gaining patience and wisdom you didn't know you possessed.

A small shift toward acceptance occurred when I realized that, even though he had diabetes, Brennan was the same child he had always been. I had been raised to look at people with disabilities as different, as less than perfect beings. I had to adjust my limited vision of perfection for myself and for my son. I had been so proud of his perfect health and now that no longer existed. I suddenly saw that he was still "perfect"; it was just that his "perfectness" now included diabetes.

One father expressed his acceptance this way: "Everyone is handicapped in some way. Some handicaps are visible; some are not. A handicap, any handicap, is just a uniqueness, something all your own. I try to share that concept with my daughter by explaining that diabetes is not something she is, but something she has. She hasn't been singled out or punished by God; she is unique and worthwhile. Her diabetes is just one facet of all that makes her so."

The truth is that your child's diabetes is here to stay (until we find the cure), and nonacceptance will not change that. Let go of the final walls that stand between you and acceptance. If you're having trouble doing that on your own, talk with someone who understands such as your spouse, another parent, or a professional. Be gentle with yourself, especially if your child has only recently been diagnosed. Acceptance is reached after the process of grieving has been completed. You'll get there.

Confusion

You may experience a period of confusion. You feel as if you've been asked to become a nurse/dietitian/diabetes expert in a very short period of time. In a sense, you have. You can help yourself by remembering that you have experts on whom you can call. If your family is in the midst of additional sources of upheaval, you have even more reason to feel overwhelmed. One family wrote me that their four-year-old son was "diagnosed in April, we had a new baby in May, and moved into a new house in June. So what's a little pressure?" Yet, they got through all the chaos and so can you.

You may also be confused about how much of a role you should take in your child's care versus how much your child should do. For example, your teen still wants you to load his shot, but doesn't want to be nagged about his blood tests, or your ten-year-old doesn't want to give himself shots. The solution depends on your child's age, level of maturity, and willingness, and can be determined with the help of diabetes experts and your own common sense. The fun part is that just about the time everything settles into a nice, predictable pattern, your child will grow to a new level of maturity and you'll need to adjust.

Balancing your family's needs will cause confusion at times. A family is not unlike a mobile hanging suspended in midair. If you move one part of the mobile, all the others move to counterbalance that movement. Your family has been thrown out of alignment by diabetes, and it takes effort to find a new pattern into which to settle. Your nondiabetic children may resent the time you spend hovering over the diabetic sibling. The diabetic child might resent that he has to follow a diet and have shots when no one else does.

And there you are, stuck in the middle, wanting everyone to be happy. Of course, you can't change the diagnosis and you can't make everybody happy. You can listen to their feelings and, in return, ask them to listen to yours. Let them know you understand how difficult these changes are for them. Do the best you can do. Don't worry, that will be good enough.

STRESSED OUT

Earlier, I wrote of being willing to get go of some of your expectations. You will, however, need to add one expectation. Expect diabetes to be stressful, especially in the beginning. Accept that sometimes all the changes are going to feel like too much to handle. Don't think you shouldn't feel like you can't take one more minute or one more day. There's nothing wrong with feeling whatever it is you're going through. Feeling deeply, be it positive or negative, is a sign of being truly, richly human. People pay hard-earned money to see actors portray intense moments of human drama in part because it feels good to feel deeply about something. So look at the bright side; you have all the intensity you can handle for free!

To paraphrase M. Scott Peck in *The Road Less Traveled*, life is difficult, and when we accept that it is, it (the difficulty) no longer matters. There is much talk of stress these days. The key to dealing with stress is to become aware of what's bothering you and why, and then to have an approach that helps diminish the resulting stress.

Let's suppose you're afraid that there's going to be an emergency and you're not going to be able to handle it properly. Instead of feeling paralyzed by a general fear, be more specific. What exactly are you afraid of? Are you afraid that your child will die because of your inability to act appropriately? I remember feeling that way. If that's your fear, talk to your doctor or educator at length about emergencies and what might happen if you failed to do such and such. Get all the information you can. Have someone put you through a trial run of treating a low blood sugar seizure with liquid glucose or glucagon. Talk to other parents about the emergencies they've been through. We all made it and so did our children.

If your stresses are caused by practical concerns, educate yourself—you can never know too much about diabetes. If stress is caused by your feelings, create safe places to deal with those emotions. There are two ways to create those safe places: one is to do it for yourself, the other is to get others to assist you. First, let's look at what you can do, through the use of visualization, writing, relaxation techniques, laughter, and prayer to lessen the stress of living with diabetes.

Picture This

The mind is a powerful tool that works either for or against you. The mind will do what you train it to do. Each of us has developed certain ways of thinking about our lives and the way the world works. Some of us have an anxious way of thinking while some of us have calm ways. The ways of your mind are not beyond your control. Thoughts emerge from learned patterns and can be changed or, at the very least, modified. Also, your body reacts to what the mind is thinking. When your mind fills your head with stressful talk, make the choice to take a vacation from it.

Visualization is a technique of using your mind to create a picture of something not presently in your sight. It's a lovely way to relieve stress and mitigate the effects of difficult emotions. Close your eyes and remember a time and a place where you were perfectly relaxed. For me, it is a particular morning in Hawaii when I floated in gentle waves at the edge of the beach. I can smell the warm air, feel the sensuous water supporting me. Just by seeing that morning sky and re-creating that scene, I can feel my body let go. Perhaps you can easily recall a time when all was right in your life. You can take an excursion to that calm feeling anytime you want.

Or you might try visualizing an abstract experience which you have not yet known. What would it be like to float on a cloud? To allow the cloud to totally support you and hold you in its soft embrace? Try picturing a circumstance in which you feel totally loved and relaxed. The words alone can assist you in relaxing, but you will enjoy the fullest effect by creating the picture in your mind's eye.

As an actress, I have learned that the body will believe what we tell it. That's basically what acting is—creating the feelings we need to portray by talking the body into feeling them. If I talk to myself in a focused manner by way of words and pictures about an emotion, I will begin to feel it.

You can use this same technique to get away from the elements that, for you, are stressful. It's really just a form of self-hypnosis. There are also wonderful relaxation audiotapes available that you can play in your car or just before you go to sleep. I used one during a particularly difficult time of my life and found it very helpful. I got mine from a "New Age" bookstore, but they are now widely available. I've listed the address of the company that produced that tape in the Resources section.

With Pen in Hand

Another simple and effective tool for dealing with feelings and the resulting stress is writing. The act of putting thoughts and feelings on paper allows us to step back and take an objective look at them. It also helps us in clarifying what we really feel, if we allow our pens to connect directly to our hearts and do not censor what appears.

You might try keeping a journal that will become a running commentary on your life. Some community colleges have journal writing classes to assist you in getting started. You might try writing when there is no one for you to talk to. But, even if you have good friends to hear your words, writing can open up new avenues for self-examination.

My life used to contain an amazing amount of chaos, which would sometimes begin to overwhelm me. I remember, on many occasions, pouring all my pent-up anger and frustration onto page after page of notebook paper. The feelings I wrote were too terrible to tell anyone (or so I thought). Yet, once upon the page, they seemed manageable. I would most often take these negative ramblings and throw them in the trash (a symbolic, as well as practical, gesture). I always felt relieved and much more in control after such a session. I highly recommend it!

Laughter and Lifesavers

There has been a continuing debate among various branches of the scientific community as to whether the mind affects the body more or vice versa. Let's assume that both are true and use every method we can to deal with difficulties in our lives. We've looked at a few techniques for assisting our mental attitude. Now let's see what you can do to make your body change your state of mind.

The first suggestion may seem a little obvious and trivial, but it does work. Smile. Even if you feel like everything's just gone down the old "Tidy Bowl," show those pearly whites. Rent an Abbott and Costello film, turn on *America's Funniest Videos,* or whatever gets the chuckles started. Norman Cousins wrote *Anatomy of an Illness* about his experience of conquering a serious, debilitating disease partially through the use of laughter. Laughter won't take away the diabetes, but it will lighten the burden.

There is an actual physiological reason for this. Studies indicate that a flow of warm blood to the brain is associated with unpleasant feelings and the flow of cooler blood with pleasant feelings. As facial muscles tighten in a smile, they constrict the blood flow to the sinus area, through which the main blood supply flows to the brain. This decrease cools the sinuses and thus the blood flowing through them to the brain. At the same time, smiling changes your breathing pattern, allowing more air to flow through the nasal passages, which also contributes to cooling the sinuses. Psychologist Robert Zajonc of the University of Michigan says, "If you can cool the brain temporarily, you'll experience a positive feeling. You can do this by smiling, by breathing techniques, or by directly infusing colder air into the nasal passage, as we did experimentally. Yoga, meditation, biofeedback, and Lamaze breathing aren't magic. They work because the patient changes breathing patterns or facial expression in a way that alters brain temperature to allow for a release of endorphins in the brain that reduce pain."

The more you smile, the better you'll feel, and the better you feel . . . you get the picture. Remember times when you've tried to cheer up your child? You smiled and thought of reasons to be happy. You probably influenced your own state of mind as much as your child's!

You'll find, as time goes on, that diabetes will provide a few laughs. A story told to me by Brennan's school bus driver, Annie, brings on my favorite diabetes-related laughter. Brennan would sometimes get low during the afternoon ride home. Annie always carried Lifesavers® candies, just in case. One of the other students on the bus was a boy with dyslexia, which manifested itself as a hearing difficulty. You could say a word to him and he would sometimes scramble it in his brain and hear something entirely different.

One afternoon on the way home, Brennan called up to Annie from the back of the bus, "Annie, I'm having a reaction! Pass me the Lifesavers!" She did as requested and handed the Lifesavers back to Brennan. As Brennan got off the bus, the dyslexic boy came up to Annie and asked, "Why do you give Lifesavers to Brennan when he has an erection?"

What's a Body to Do?

There's lots more body below your smile and many good techniques for getting it to relax. First, work to become aware of where you might be holding tension. The next time things get a little crazy, take a few moments to observe your body. Walk around the room and become familiar with where your body is "holding on." Say to yourself, "I allow my shoulders (or whatever part of the body) to let go and relax." Now feel the difference. With consistent practice, you'll become familiar with the way your body reacts to stress and be able to relax more quickly than before. (Also take note of the circumstance that is causing these changes and examine ways to alter the tension in that event or attitude.)

An even quicker way to deal with tension is to change your breathing. When you're in a stressful situation, your body reacts by releasing adrenaline and your breathing becomes more rapid. Your body revs up for action. You can calm down by merely forcing your breathing to be deeper and slower. Think of your breath as emanating from deep in your stomach instead of your lungs. Now, take a breath and hold it. Become aware of the space between the breaths, the place where the inhalation ends and the exhalation begins. Then let the breath out, slowly.

Try five or ten of these in a row, allowing your jaw to release and let go, creating space at the back of your mouth near your jaw hinge. Imagining a small balloon at the back of your throat will help you feel the space that exists during a yawn. Use this breathing technique frequently and become aware of the changes you feel afterward.

Exercise is a great way to reduce stress. Walking, jumping rope, swimming, and aerobic dancing are just a few of the choices. Yoga is a wonderful alternative because it will exercise your body as well as center and calm your breath. There's a wonderful yoga tape for beginners that I have listed in the Resources section.

There are lots of excuses why you might not exercise, but none of them are good ones. Toss your little one into the stroller and go. Get larger kids to ride their bikes if they don't feel like walking or running. Exercise has been used instead of drug therapy in the successful treatment of some forms of depression. Your children deserve a happy, healthy parent.

Two additional ways of letting go of body stress are biofeedback and massage. Both cost money, but can be worth it. Biofeedback involves a counselor who teaches you how to relax your body. Using technology, you are able to see how relaxed you are and which mental exercises help you become more relaxed. You practice the mental techniques until you develop the skill to be able to release tension at will. It can be very effective.

Massage is a wondrous luxury (although I know some people who consider it a necessity). A massage is a kind of professional hug. Ashley Montague speaks of the vital importance of human touch in his book, *Touching*. He relates its relevance to our mental and emotional well-being. In addition to the touching we get from family and friends, massage offers an additional source of relaxing, nourishing contact. If you can't afford to pay for a massage, bribe one of your kids into a backrub. Then complete the contact by hugging the human backrubber for as long as he'll stand for it! Or ask a good friend for a hug if you're having a tough day. Don't be shy. It feels as good to the hugger as to the huggee. Remember, you deserve it.

Some of us were brought up in families who did not do a lot of touching. I recall talking with a masseuse whose father was a fundamentalist minister who never hugged or kissed his children. As an adult she became aware that if a week went by without her giving a massage, she would become very nervous and restless. We both found it interesting that, after being raised with so little contact, she had chosen a profession which gave her permission to touch others. If you had a similar upbringing, give yourself permission to make contact.

Do all you can to be good to your body. It is the home where your heart is, and if you wear it out, you have nowhere else to live. Eat well, exercise, don't smoke, drink little, wear your seat belt. Take time for yourself. A dear friend in Ohio arranged with her family to have a once-a-month "Susie Day." They would see what money could be spared, sometimes only $10, and she would take off for the day. Sometimes she would see a movie or just sit in the park and read. When she got home, she was refreshed and grateful for her family's understanding.

The Highest Perspective

Most of us have been raised with some religious training. We may or may not have continued in that particular system of belief as we grew up. Perhaps formal religion was not a good experience for you. You can still get beyond the letter of the (religious) law to its spirit.

That has been my experience. I was raised within a rigid religious context that was like an exclusive club of sorts. (If you don't believe as we believe, you go to hell.) That didn't work for me. I could not possibly believe that God had such a limited heart. That approach caused me to leave spirituality out of my life for many years. Yet, I longed to have a working relationship with God and just recently I have turned to my belief in a Greater Power and found deep wells of comfort.

As I look back, I see that everything I've encountered (no matter how painful it seemed at the time) has contributed to my growth and to greater understanding. I find this outlook to be of great value to me, allowing me to accept everything that comes my way with a certain equanimity. It leads me to accept that, perhaps, from the highest perspective (the Absolute), there is a good reason for everything that happens.

Having faith in this view of life gives me great comfort and inner peace. It is a blessing to be able to turn problems over to God and really trust that their resolution will be for the best. A few quiet moments of prayer spent in asking for help and strength can lighten the burden. After asking, a few extra moments spent in a state of receptivity can perhaps provide the answers sought.

Another form of prayer is meditation. Meditation can be spiritual or secular in context. Meditation is a process of stilling the activity of the mind by focusing on one point. That point might be a word or phrase. It might be focusing on the breath or the space in between each breath. Meditation is a private enterprise, the goal of which is to experience an inner center—a larger Self.

I began meditating a year ago and have felt my life shift in a perceptible way toward a peacefulness I had never known before. It is another tool at your disposal to help you stay calm and steady in the midst of the demands of parenthood and life in general. In the Resources section I've listed a few books and tapes to get you started.

Spirituality and prayer are a personal issue. I discuss it to remind you of its possible usefulness in case you have not recently sought its assistance.

All these techniques are suggestions to help you deal with the demands of raising a child with a chronic illness. The better shape you're in, the better you're able to care for your child. The "selfishness" of taking time to care for your own needs is essential to your being the best parent you can be for your child.

FIRM SUPPORT

What we want to give to our children we need to create for ourselves: a support system where feelings are listened to nonjudgmentally, where people who care about you reach out to help you. Maybe asking for help or expressing anger has been difficult for you. You can change that. You can learn to deal constructively with the changes and stresses of living with diabetes and apply those techniques to other areas of your life.

We have looked at some of the ways you can take care of yourself. Now let's widen the circle and see who else you might have help you: the members of your immediate family, close relatives, friends and neighbors, baby-sitters, and support groups.

Mother's Helper

I'm going to assume that the person reading this book is a mother. In spite of the changes brought about by women working outside the home, many more women than men still provide the primary care for their children. It is, however, very important that a father take an active role in his child's diabetes care right from the beginning. If a father has not taken the time to become knowledgeable or assist in the practical aspects of care, the child may think that diabetes is not all that important.

Some fathers are wonderful about sharing the job of caring for a diabetic child. Some require an extra push now and then. A father who declines to actively participate in his child's diabetes care may need to see a counselor to work through the feelings that are blocking his participation.

It's hard for me to imagine any father having no involvement. It is not so difficult, however, to imagine that in many families almost all the responsibility is mom's. (Perhaps because that's what it was like for me.)

Psychiatrist Dr. David Viscott recently said, "The most important thing a father can do for his children is to love their mother." Loving means more than affection. It also means extending oneself to help and support the loved one.

If you're the mom, become aware of how much you do. Do you plan the meals, cook them, do the blood tests, give the shots, keep the records, and do all the planning for emergencies? Did you help create this role for yourself by thinking you need to do it all, that you are the only one who can do it right? Have you not asked for help because you have trouble doing that or because it causes too many problems?

Interpersonal relationships are very tricky. Once they're established and the rules seem set, it's not always easy to introduce new ways of doing things. Diabetes has thrown you all a curve anyway, so while you're in the midst of upheaval, it might be a good time to make one or two more changes.

You and your spouse may have set the balance of power and division of labor before your child's diabetes, and it was acceptable to you. Maybe you need more help now. Nobody will read your mind, so speak up and ask for help.

It is better that the responsibility for the care of the diabetic member not fall squarely on one person's shoulders. The involvement of the whole family gives the diabetic child the feeling that he is accepted and loved, even though diabetes has added complications to his family's life.

Siblings

If your diabetic child is not an only child, you will find yourself having to handle the many feelings and behaviors that siblings have about what diabetes has brought into their lives. Their feelings may cause you some concern and difficulty, especially in the early stages, but once the necessary adjustments are made, siblings can be a wonderful source of support.

Parents of a newly diagnosed child worry that their other children will resent all the time and attention given to the diabetic child. You can avoid resentment by making sure siblings are included in the changes your family is experiencing. Get your other children to participate in the diabetes care routine and create opportunities for them to help. They can assist by distracting a younger one during the shot or blood test or help treat an insulin reaction. They will feel good about being helpful, and their assistance will discourage feelings of being left out.

Many times, siblings don't understand the seriousness of diabetes until they see a severe insulin reaction. Several parents I know have reported a definite change for the better in siblings' attitudes after such an incident. Teaching siblings how to handle a reaction will make them feel valuable and give you the opportunity to let them know how important their help is. It will also help decrease any anxiety they may feel.

Siblings' feelings may manifest as negative behavior. In a younger sibling, that behavior may take the form of regression. Rather than treat babyish actions by the Joan Rivers method (Oh, grow up!), use hugs and extra attention to placate the injured party. We all need a little extra baby-ing now and then.

Whether your nondiabetic child exhibits negative behavior or not, be aware that some feelings of resentment are to be expected. You can calm those feelings by making special efforts to concentrate on what will make that child feel good about himself and his relationship to you. Plan a small outing together. Something as simple as a shopping trip because "I really need your help" can really make a difference. Let your child overhear you telling someone how wonderful he is at———. Acknowledge his efforts and accomplishments every chance you get.

Fears may crop up. Your nondiabetic child may be afraid that he too will get diabetes. You can reassure him that the odds of that happening are low. Also, just as some diabetic children believe that their diabetes is a pun-ishment for being "bad," siblings may feel they caused the diabetes by thinking "bad" thoughts about their brothers or sisters. If you suspect this to be the case, you can explain what causes diabetes in an age-appropriate manner and assure your child that there is no way he could have possibly caused his sibling's diabetes.

Your child needs to know that he is just as important as ever, even though he doesn't have diabetes. Take time to listen to the hard feelings he may harbor. You know that you can't "fix" the source of the feelings, but you can "make it better" by listening sympathetically.

Look at the bright side. The extra time you spend with your diabetic child plus the time you spend with other siblings to compensate for the time you spend with your diabetic child add up to lots of family together-ness. As one father said, "I never knew Walt Disney made so many movies!"

Little by little, siblings adjust to having diabetes in their families' lives. The same techniques of listening with love and sympathetic understand-ing that you use with your diabetic child will help your other children make the transition to acceptance.

All in the Family

As a parent who has been through a diabetes education course, you now have the tools with which to educate other family members. If they are willing, they can learn to give shots and blood tests as well as support your child's diet plan. Grandparents, in particular, can play a very important role.

If your child's grandparents do not live close by, you can at least send them pamphlets and perhaps a book that will help them understand what your child and family are going through. If they live nearby, they can become involved in a more immediate way.

Keep in mind that the grandparents may be experiencing some of the same feelings that you are as a parent, such as loss, sadness, denial, anger. They may doubt their ability to properly care for your child now that he has diabetes. Talk with them about how you need their help and support and how you hope they will participate. Include them in taking over some of the diabetes care routine when you are together. That way you can build their confidence slowly without their feeling that they have to be responsible all at once.

Education and experience will help grandparents and other family members who have a hands-on relationship with your child to feel comfortable and be more understanding. Check with your doctor or diabetes educator to see if there is a class or workshop they can attend in order to educate themselves. The American Diabetes Association has many such classes. There is even a camp in Maine called Camp Grand especially for diabetic children and their grandparents.

You may find that some family members will not want to be involved in your child's diabetes care. That will be disappointing to you, to say the least. One mother told me that her child's grandparents refuse to learn about diabetes or participate in her child's care.

If this is the case for you, you can try talking with them. Most likely their refusal stems from fear—fear that they cannot learn what is necessary, that they might do something wrong and hurt their grandchild—the same fears you have had. The difference is that you had to get over your fears in order for your child to go on living and they don't have to do so.

Give them a chance to talk about their fears. Let them know you've felt the same. Discuss the expectations each of you hold. See if you can negotiate with them. Would they learn a little about the diet and be willing to support your child's diet plan? Would they learn to do a blood test? Let them know that you want their grandchild to be able to spend time alone with them, but that won't be possible unless certain of your child's basic needs are met.

If they still refuse to participate, let it go. Know that it is their loss. You need to forgive them, no matter how angry and hurt you feel, so that your child will not think that he and his diabetes caused the tension between you. Let them be with your child in the ways in which they are capable and willing. Look to other sources of support.

Friends and Neighbors

The wider circle of your friends and neighbors will also need to know some basic facts about diabetes and how it affects your child so that they can support his meal plan, as well as recognize and assist with an insulin reaction if necessary. If your child is uncomfortable about everyone knowing or his diabetes being treated as a big deal, ask those you inform to be very low-key about the subject in front of him.

There are going to be questions from people who do not understand what diabetes is or why your child has to take injections when, for example, their Aunt Sadie only took a pill. A simple explanation of the difference between Type 1 and Type 2 diabetes will be required. Try something such as, "Your Aunt Sadie had non-insulin dependent diabetes. Her body was still producing insulin, but it either wasn't producing quite enough insulin, or the insulin wasn't being used efficiently. She was taking pills which stimulated her body to produce or use her own insulin effectively. On the other hand, my child has insulin-dependent diabetes. The cells in his pancreas that produce insulin have been destroyed. Insulin is essential for life, so we must inject it into him every day in order for him to be healthy."

You may be asked why the term *juvenile* diabetes is used. I have even heard it mistakenly referred to as "junior" diabetes, as if it were a pint-sized version of the real thing. You can explain that insulin-dependent, or Type 1, diabetes used to be called "juvenile" diabetes because it is usually diagnosed before the age of thirty. Let them know that it is the severest form of the disease and that people with Type 1 do not outgrow it.

You will have to spend some time educating people in your life about diabetes, but the time is definitely worthwhile. It is heartwarming to see the extra effort some people will extend once they understand what diabetes means for your child and your family.

One diabetic girl named Megan sings in her church's "Candy Choir" that is composed of children aged three years and up and performs for special revival meetings. At the end of the evening service, all the children are given candy. The first time Megan sang, her mother whisked her away immediately after the program so that she wouldn't see the other children get their candy. She called the pastor's wife to let her know why. The next time Megan sang in the choir, the pastor's wife gave her a small stuffed dog after the service. From then on, they always had a sugarless treat especially for Megan. Her mother commented, "It made me feel so good that they took the effort required to include her and reward her with something she can have."

Sometimes, others we try to educate don't quite get it. One mom found herself upset with a neighbor who continually allowed her children to come over with cookies and candy. She told the children that sugared treats were not allowed in her house. She began keeping a supply of sugar-free gum, candy, Fudgsicles™, and Jell-O on hand for all the kids. They now look forward to coming over to her house. "They all love the treats. It's expensive to feed everyone, but it's worth it." She also gives them a quick lesson in diabetes management and supplies them with needleless syringes and used blood test strips to use on their dolls and stuffed animals.

Patience and a generous approach paid off in both instances.

My Kingdom for a Sitter!

Anyone who cares for your child in your home needs to be thoroughly educated in diabetes management. The baby-sitter needs all the information that you normally work with: how to take tests and give shots (if they will be required), the meal plan, how to recognize and treat reactions, phone numbers for you and any and all medical personnel who might be helpful, and the paramedics (just in case). It may ease your mind to know that in the twelve years my son has had diabetes we have not once had to call the paramedics. You should also tell the baby-sitter any of your child's idiosyncrasies relating to diabetes, such as his particular symptoms for an oncoming reaction and the times or circumstances when reactions are most likely to occur.

Take the sitter through a rehearsal of what to do during a reaction. You want to be certain that the sitter is being watchful for a reaction and has a sugar source close at hand. Have her use a sugar source, such as liquid glucose, cake frosting in a tube, or honey, which can be administered whether or not your child is conscious. Of course, you will have these things readily available, but having the sitter actually go through the motions will make both of you feel more confident.

If you're only going out for the evening, you can check your child's blood sugar before you leave. That will give you an idea of what's going on. For example, if it's before the shot and dinner is not quite ready and your child is showing a low reading, you might want to delay leaving until you know the blood sugar is at a normal level and the shot is given and dinner is on the table. Many parents, especially in the first year after diagnosis or with a very small child, feel much calmer about leaving after the dinner hour is over and they know that the child has eaten.

Some parents, however, are so fearful that they don't go out at all. I received a letter from two parents who were grappling with their fears. "We haven't been away from our child since she was diagnosed. We need a break, but we're afraid to leave her with anyone else."

They're right; they deserve a break. They may actually know people who are perfectly capable of taking care of their diabetic child, yet their fear immobilizes them. They need some reassurance that others can be educated to care for their child just as they were. They could start small, perhaps with dinner and a movie close to home, and provide the sitter with phone numbers of both locations. It's a good idea for them to call in every hour or so to see how things are going. I have a feeling they'll spend much of their first evening away on the phone!

They could also invest in a beeper. Several parents I talked with decided to carry a beeper so that they were instantly available in case of questions or problems. Being that accessible gave them peace of mind and helped their children's caretakers breathe easier, too.

You can locate baby-sitters through a good baby-sitting agency by letting them know you want someone familiar with diabetes and through recommendations from the ADA and the JDF chapters nearest you, as well as other parents. A local nursing school can often give names of students who baby-sit. Also, your doctor might have a diabetic teenager as a patient whom you could talk into baby-sitting for you.

With time and patience, you can develop a broad-based baby-sitting support system, with family, friends, other parents, and a trained sitter or two who occasionally give you a time away. Another alternative is for you and your spouse to take turns giving each other a night out with friends.

If you must go out of town and your child is newly diagnosed, you might try what I once did. Shortly after Brennan was diagnosed, his father and I had a trip we could not cancel. I had a housekeeper who was very capable and friends who were going to stop by to see that everything was running smoothly, but no one was quite ready to take on giving Brennan's injections. We decided to hire a nurse to stop by in the morning and at dinnertime to give the shot and check on the test data. It was expensive, but luckily we could afford it. It gave us peace of mind to know that a professional was overseeing our son's care.

Through the years, until Brennan began giving his own shots, almost everyone who worked with us (housekeepers and secretaries), as well as several of our friends, learned to give injections. We never had a mishap.

Support Groups

In a letter to me, a father wrote, "It's so important to be with people who really understand what we need to do every day to keep our children healthy." That is what you get when you join a support group—people who really understand. There is no one who understands what you are going through better than another parent. In addition to giving you a safe, understanding arena in which to air your feelings, a support group gives you a chance to swap coping techniques and practical advice.

One mother, whose daughter was diagnosed at age fifteen months, phoned a support group the night she checked her child into the hospital.

"That was the best phone call I could have made. I still rely on the give and take of our support group as much as I did the first time I attended."

Another function of a support group is to start a baby-sitting co-op and take turns caring for each other's children so that parents can have a night or two away without fear. One father remarked, "It's great to be able to leave instructions about shots, tests, etc., and know that they'll be carried out with care and precision."

If you're not in a support group, call the ADA or JDF to see what's available in your area. If there's no group available, start one of your own. Talk with a few diabetes doctors and educators and ask them if they'll let their clients know your intention. Make a simple flyer that they can hand out or leave in their waiting rooms.

SCHOOL DAZE

It's essential to educate your child's caretakers while they're educating your child. Their being able to effectively handle your child's medical needs will add greatly to your peace of mind.

You will need to educate all of your child's school caretakers: the teachers, school nurse, cafeteria manager, and bus driver. They need to know what happens when your child has an insulin reaction and what they should do about it. Make sure they have juice, crackers, and liquid glucose of some sort available to treat reactions. You should keep some blood testing equipment with the school nurse.

Most likely, you will not encounter any difficulty in getting your child's needs met. You may, however, have to take some initiative. One mother arranged a small group meeting and showed a video, "Energy Is Life" (listed in the Resources section). She felt it had a positive effect on the understanding and support her child received. Another mom signed up as room-mother so that she could influence the foods served for class parties and snacks. At another school, no snack was served, so the parent sent graham crackers for everyone. You and the teacher can decide how best to handle the snack your child needs.

You might encounter resistance to keeping your child's blood testing equipment at school. One mother was told that school officials were worried that the equipment had something to do with drugs and drug abuse. People fear diabetes because they don't understand it. If necessary, get your doctor or nurse-educator to call or send a note explaining that the equipment is essential to your child's care. As well as the video I previously mentioned, both JDF and ADA have pamphlets that explain diabetes to teachers and school personnel.

One mother, Roxanne, had to go to extraordinary lengths to get her school to cooperate. They would not allow her daughter to take her noon shot at school and refused to assist in other aspects of her care. "I initiated a complaint with the Illinois State Board of Education requesting under state law that my daughter was eligible for services as a handicapped (health-impaired) child. I had to endure three hearings and one appeal before I achieved success. The state of Illinois forced the school to develop an emergency plan acceptable to her doctor for handling hypoglycemic episodes at school. These hearings were difficult, as the school's attorney attempted to discredit me and downplay the severity of insulin shock.

"I also filed a complaint with the U.S. Department of Education, Office of Civil Rights, to further force her school to cooperate with her daily needs, which included the noon injection. Section 504 of the Rehabilitation Act of 1974 provides protection for people with diabetes, asthma, epilepsy, etc.

"There is a widespread problem of diabetic children being medically neglected in schools. If parents don't know their rights and how to exert them, their diabetic kids are at the mercy of schools who refuse to care for their medical needs while at school, even though they are required to under state and federal laws."

She was finally able to get the school to comply with her daughter's medical needs. Other children and parents have not been so lucky.

One child in Oklahoma wound up hospitalized for nine days for severe insulin shock because her teacher would not let her have her snack and then refused to excuse her from class to treat her low blood sugar. She finally understood that there was a problem when the child passed out.

A girl in Pennsylvania was barred from attending school unless her mother was with her, merely because she was diabetic.

Another boy was denied permission to perform blood tests at school.

These cases are extreme examples. They seem to happen more often in small rural districts, but can happen in urban communities. There are ways to ensure that your child enjoys full rights under the law.

BECOMING AN ADVOCATE

It is amazing what one person can accomplish when she fully commits her heart and mind to something. I have certainly seen commitment change the context and purpose of my life. Yet I am by no means special. There are so many parents who accomplish much in the name of their children.

Roxanne, the woman who filed complaints with the state and federal government, was doing so in the midst of an intense personal crisis. Her husband had just walked out on the family, the furnace was broken, and there was no money and no car. She had two small children living at home, one with cerebral palsy and one with diabetes. Yet she managed to get through it all. The family now has a new furnace and a car, she has two part-time jobs, plus she raises Border collies and illustrates books at home. (As far as I'm concerned, she qualifies for "Goddess of the Year!")

Roxanne did all of that because she loves her children and is willing to fight to give them the best of herself. We all want to be the best we can be for our children. Sometimes that means reaching out beyond the walls of our homes and our children's schools.

One mother wrote to me, "We need something to give us all that inner strength to face the insensitivity that is out there in the world. We don't want to create barriers between ourselves and the outside world."

To me, the key to her worry about feeling isolated is the phrase "the outside world." In a sense, she has created the feeling of isolation by seeing herself as separate and different from everyone else and jumping them all into one category called "the outside world." She would be wise to remember that not too long ago she also didn't know anything about diabetes—that she was also one of the "outsiders."

Insensitivity is often born of ignorance, but, in the case of diabetes, it's an understandable ignorance. There's really no good reason that people should know very much about diabetes unless it has touched their lives. As parents of diabetic children, we have the chance to transform ignorance into empathy by becoming an advocate for diabetes. An *advocate* is defined as one who pleads another's cause, and that is exactly what we do for our children when we educate or inform others. By taking on the responsibility of being a public relations expert on behalf of diabetes, we feel less victimized by insensitivity.

The more we reach out and share what we know, the stronger we are, not only for ourselves but also for our children.

Here are some of the things you can do:

1.   Learn everything you can about diabetes. Use the Resources section to become familiar with the resources available to you.
2.   Join a support group.

3. Join the two major diabetes organizations, the Juvenile Diabetes Foundation International and the American Diabetes Association. They both publish excellent magazines that you receive as part of your membership.

4. Educate others, especially all the people who have regular contact with your child.

5. Raise money to find a cure. Both JDF and ADA raise money for research. As a parent, my primary goal is to find a cure for diabetes.

6. If your child is being denied his rights under the law, which translates as being denied access to appropriate diabetes care while at school, do something about it.

The federal Education for All Handicapped Children's Act (PL 94-142) states that handicapped children are entitled to a public education, appropriate to their needs, at no cost to their families and that they must be provided the services they need in order to benefit from the educational program. In addition, Section 504 of the Rehabilitation Act (PL 93-112) guarantees that people with disabilities may not be discriminated against because of their disability, which encompasses the right to vote, education, accessibility, employment, and other rights. Because your child has diabetes, he qualifies as health impaired under this law.

There is an organization called TASK, Teams of Advocates for Special Kids, which can help you guarantee your child's rights under the law. Your child has the right to special services that assist his functioning at school. That means the school should cooperate in allowing him to test his blood, give his shot (if necessary), and appropriately treat insulin reactions.

TASK was begun by Terri Boies, a nurse who has three children with learning disabilities. It informs and trains parents so that they can use the federal laws to assure their children are treated fairly. They have a Parent Training Project that is funded in part through a U.S. Department of

Education grant. TASK operates out of Orange County, California, and provides parent-to-parent support groups, resource and referral information, educational workshops, legal rights information, telephone advocacy, a speaker's bureau, and a newsletter.

If you're having trouble getting your child's needs met at school, I suggest you call TASK at 714-533-TASK or write them at 100 W. Cerritos Ave., Anaheim, CA 92805. Speak with Terri Boies or Project Coordinator Marta Anchondo.

COURSE CORRECTION

Each of our lives is founded on a belief system. Those beliefs form the basis of our expectations. Of course, nothing is ever what we expect it to be. We are constantly reassessing our expectations, making course corrections.

The diagnosis of your child's diabetes has necessitated a major course correction, jolting you to a new way of living, and new levels of knowledge and understanding. Challenging you to extend yourself, it provides an opportunity to adjust your priorities, to be more aware of the fragility of life. It requires that you learn even better ways of taking care of yourself and those you love, that you become a teacher and an advocate for diabetes.

Sometimes it requires more of you than you believe yourself capable. Yet, like most challenges, the rewards are commensurate with the love and hard work you invest. Seeing your child gain maturity and self-discipline while responsibly caring for his diabetes is a source of great satisfaction. If you are just starting down this long road of raising a child with diabetes, take it from those of us who have been traveling it for many years—you and your child will do just fine!

7

Research Moves Toward a Cure

Brennan no longer asks me when his shots will be over as he did when he was four years old. He knows and accepts that his diabetes will not simply disappear—it will take more than that.

The "more than that" is a promise I have made. I have told my son that I will find a cure for his diabetes. It is not an idle promise, and it is not a promise that I make alone.

I have been the Celebrity Chairman for the Juvenile Diabetes Foundation International for several years now. I have seen the incredible growth of this organization and its commitment to fund research in order to find the answers we need.

That commitment took on new meaning in 1990, which marked the twentieth anniversary of JDF and the beginning of the "Decade for the Cure." We at JDF have designated the last ten years of the twentieth century as the final march toward the ultimate answer—a cure for diabetes. It is our vision that a cure is possible if adequate funds are allocated for research.

To say we can cure diabetes is an outrageous thing to do. Yet JDF has been talking about finding a cure for the past twenty years, long before anyone else thought it was possible. We have talked with the researchers and they tell us that they can provide the answers within the next ten years if enough money is committed to research.

How much money is enough? Enough means sufficient funds to underwrite all the meritorious grant applications received from the scientific community. At present, because of insufficient funds, JDF can fund only one out of five researchers who want to do worthwhile research in diabetes. The U.S. government funds only one out of four researchers. That means that 75 to 80 percent of the scientists who would like to be working on diabetes-related questions are not able to obtain funding from JDF or the U.S. government, the two largest sources of diabetes research funding in the world.

A cure can be found. During President Franklin Delano Roosevelt's term of office, a commitment was made to find a cure for polio. It became a priority and the task was accomplished. The same thing happened after John F. Kennedy inspired us all to believe that we could put a man on the moon. In the same way, with commitment and the proper allocation of resources, we can make diabetes a thing of the past.

This chapter delineates the course and substance of diabetes research, how far we've come, and how much farther we have left to travel. This information is a gift of hope to encourage you to become involved in raising the money we need to end diabetes once and for all.

A HISTORY OF DIABETES

The first known written record of diabetes was set down on papyrus thirty-five centuries ago. Drafted in 1500 B.C. by an Egyptian medical scribe, it contained advice for the treatment of frequent urination (one of the symptoms of diabetes).

Then, in 100 A.D., Aretaeus of Cappadocia, a Greek physician, gave diabetes its name. The word *diabetes* means "siphon," relating to the draining of the body's liquids through frequent urination.

In the sixteenth century, the European physician Paracelsus made note of a residue of white powder in the evaporated urine of a diabetic patient. He mistook it for salt, but it was actually sugar.

Then, a century later, because of the sweetness of a diabetic's urine, the Latin word for honey was added to the medical term for diabetes and it became known as diabetes mellitus. Also in the seventeenth century, Johann Conrad Brunner removed the pancreas from dogs and noted their thirst and frequent urination. Unfortunately, he failed to connect their symptoms to diabetes.

In the 1700s, an Englishman named Thomas Cawley demonstrated the presence of sugar in the urine. Five years after his first discovery he performed an autopsy on a diabetic and noticed that the pancreas appeared to be different from that of a healthy person. Since he believed that diabetes was a disease of the kidneys, Cawley chose not to investigate his findings.

The 1800s witnessed valuable progress. A German medical student named Paul Langerhans found clusters of cells within the pancreas that differed from other pancreatic cells. They were named the "islets of Langerhans." Also during this century, J. von Mering and Oscar Minkowitz managed to keep a dog alive after removing its pancreas. The animal quickly developed symptoms identical to those of a human diabetic. They repeated the procedure with other dogs and obtained similar results. Because of their work, the pancreas was finally linked to diabetes.

Eugene L. Opie performed autopsies on diabetic patients in 1902 and discovered degeneration of the islets of Langerhans. In 1907, two researchers made a distinction between two types of islet cells and called them Type A (alpha) and Type B (beta).

J. Homan identified the beta cells as the source of a hormone called insulin in 1916. At about the same time, Sir Edward Sharpey-Schafer suggested that the metabolism of carbohydrates is controlled by a substance produced in the islets.

1921 was a revolutionary year for diabetes research. In Toronto, Dr. Frederick Banting and his medical assistant, Charles Best, administered a pure extract of insulin to dogs, and then to a human diabetic, eleven-year-old Leonard Thompson. Leonard had been on a restricted diet because of his diabetes and weighed only 75 pounds. The insulin lowered his blood sugar. The injections were continued and he lived to maturity, which was not then the case with diabetic children.

Banting and Best also treated a diabetic physician, Joseph Gilchrist, with insulin, sometimes causing insulin shock. Dr. Gilchrist was able to describe in scientific detail an account of insulin shock from the experience of the diabetic—a first.

Although insulin did not provide a cure, it did drastically change the lives of diabetics. Instead of a life shortened and terrorized by diabetes, diabetics were able, with daily insulin injections, to lead relatively normal lives with considerably extended life expectancies.

Since the discovery of insulin, advances in research have increased exponentially. In 1936, a Danish doctor, Hans Christian Hagedorn, discovered that protamine zinc combined with insulin enabled a constant and prolonged absorption of the hormone.

In 1950, a test was perfected that enabled scientists to measure insulin levels in the blood, providing them with evidence that some diabetics have insulin circulating in their blood and some have none.

Dr. Donald Steiner discovered in 1965 that insulin begins as a single chain molecule, which he named prosulin. The prosulin is then converted to insulin, a double chain molecule with a connecting protein bridge, in the beta cells.

In 1971, a prototypical artificial pancreas was developed.

Vitrectomy was developed in 1972. Diabetes causes hemorrhages that cloud the fluid that fills the eye, resulting in severe vision loss. In vitrectomy, a suction-drill device removes the clouded fluid and replaces it with clear liquid, improving the vision of diabetics dramatically.

The discovery, purification, and synthesis of glucagon and somatostatin (two hormones produced by the pancreas which affect blood sugar levels) in 1973 marked another step toward understanding the factors that alter the effect of insulin.

In 1974, antibodies hostile to the islets were detected in insulin-dependent diabetics. Then, evidence was found that indicated a possible connection between viruses and the onset of diabetes.

Since then, the discoveries and progress have been truly amazing. All of these advances have added immeasurably to our ability to care for diabetic persons. Let's examine the remarkable course of recent diabetes research.

THE GENETIC RISK FACTOR

The possibility of genetic predisposition to diabetes has long been of interest to researchers. Studies have shown that relatives of diabetics have increased risk of becoming diabetic. Then, in 1975, the discovery of the HLA factor indicated that certain proteins on the surface of the cells are inherited from generation to generation. These proteins form patterns in persons with Type 1 diabetes with more frequency than in other persons. The specific pattern of these proteins is also associated with the body's immune system and adds evidence that altered immunity plays a role in causing diabetes.

HLA molecules are found on the surface of many cells that play an important role in the immune response. They bind themselves to foreign substances and identify them in a way that allows the immune system to recognize and destroy them.

One doctor discovered that nondiabetics have HLA molecules containing a certain amino acid, while 90 percent of diabetics do not. The risk associated with this single amino acid is higher than any other gene that has been linked to diabetes. The confusing element is that some people who have these "diabetes-associated" HLA genes still do not get diabetes. Researchers have begun to look for other genes and for environmental agents, such as viruses, which might also contribute to susceptibility.

In summary, diabetes is a disease born of genetic susceptibility. That means your child was born with a genetic background that makes him prone to get diabetes. This genetic defect is linked to the body's ability to recognize its own tissue as friend or foe. Not everyone with this background gets diabetes, but you will not get it if the genetic susceptibility is not present.

The genetic defect manifests in the immune system. In Type 1 diabetes, the body is fooled into identifying the beta cells as foreign invaders and produces antibodies to destroy them. Let's examine the causes of diabetes and the kinds of intervention that will be effective.

ANTIBODIES AND FRIENDS

We know that insulin-dependent diabetes occurs as the result of the destruction of beta cells (which produce insulin) within the pancreas. We also have a good idea of what causes the destruction. Immune cells, whose job it is to kill off foreign elements in the body, can be seen surrounding and infiltrating the islets (which contain the insulin-producing beta cells) shortly after diabetes is diagnosed. Because of this, scientists view diabetes as an immunologically based disease.

To appreciate what happens when diabetes occurs, we need to understand how the immune system normally works. The immune system is composed of a variety of mechanisms designed to fight off the bacteria, viruses, and tumors that threaten our bodies. Macrophages, large amoeba-like cells, patrol the bloodstream and arrive first at the site of an infection. Activated by the macrophages, T-cells send an alert to other immune cells.

Antibodies then latch onto molecules on the surface of an intruder and mark it for destruction. Lymphocytes seek out these marked, infected cells and destroy them.

Why does a system which is designed to protect our body suddenly decide to attack it? To help us understand what goes wrong, let's look at how the body normally acts.

There are three reasons why the body does not normally attack its own tissue. For one thing, most cells are capable of recognizing the body's own tissue. There are also suppressor cells, which tone down harmful immune responses. Third, tissues often have a protective mechanism of their own which makes them inaccessible or unrecognizable to immune cells. The theory is that one or more of these mechanisms fails and diabetes results. But which type of immune cell causes the damage?

The obvious candidate is the antibody. Antibodies are produced whenever the body is fighting an intruder, like an infection. It has been discovered that, at the onset of diabetes, more than 90 percent of patients have antibodies directed against their own tissues.

Another factor researchers have observed is that viruses play a part in triggering diabetes. Diagnoses of diabetes rise during flu season. Many parents have told me that their children had had the flu or some other virus several weeks before they discovered diabetes. Similarly, my son had had chicken pox seven weeks before his diagnosis.

Yet even though viruses may act as a triggering mechanism, it has become clear that the actual destruction is carried out slowly and systematically by the immune system. In 1988, researchers discovered an antibody that can predict the onset of diabetes with amazing accuracy. It is called the 64K antibody and is directed exclusively against a specific protein located on insulin-producing beta cells. Two other antibodies, ICAs (islet cell autoantibody) and IAAs (insulin autoantibody), have also been shown to be fairly reliable indicators of who will get diabetes.

It was once thought that the destruction of the beta cells was a fairly rapid process, occurring over a matter of a few months. Now it is clear that it can take as long as seven years, and that the onset of diabetes is not overt until 80 percent of the beta cells have been destroyed.

Using the discovery of these antibody indicators, investigators are developing tests that will help doctors identify people who will get diabetes long before they show signs of the disease. The next step is finding ways to stop the disease from taking hold, which is discussed in the Prevention section of this chapter. In the meantime, many developments are helping people with diabetes live healthier lives.

TREATMENTS

While many researchers around the world are seeking the causes of diabetes along with prevention and a cure, others are committed to improving the quality of life for diabetics. The list of accomplishments in the last fifteen years is impressive. Home blood glucose monitoring, laser surgery and vitrectomy to treat diabetic retinopathy and reduce the risk of blindness, innovative insulin delivery systems, and transplantation have all dramatically changed the lives of diabetics everywhere. Let's take a look at what new wonders loom on the horizon.

Computer Care

Dr. Roger Mazze, professor of epidemiology at the University of Minnesota, has pioneered computerized monitoring for diabetics. He is currently working on a practical computer software program for the primary care physician.

A program of this sort could do much to correct the sometimes haphazard nature of diabetes care from doctor to doctor. Each doctor would have available the experience of diabetologists from around the world. A doctor could feed information into the computer and it would tell her how to handle the patient—for example, whether to prescribe multiple injections, how much to prescribe at different times, or whether to start insulin therapy for a Type 2 diabetic.

A computerized diabetes control system is expected to be commercially available within a few years.

Implantable Pumps

Implantable pumps are among the newest developments. Like the insulin pump worn outside the body, they provide intensive insulin therapy and come closest to mimicking the normal functions of the pancreas.

The Programmable, Implantable Medication System (PIMS) is a spin-off of NASA space technology. The pump is about the same size as a hockey puck and is implanted under the skin of the abdomen. The patient dials a number on a handheld radio transmitter, activating a program in the computer's memory. The program tells the pump how much insulin to provide at different times of the day and stores that information for later retrieval. The pump also has built-in safety features to prevent excess delivery of insulin. It requires that the recipient keep detailed records of blood sugar tests. Based on the data that the PIMS is able to provide about hour-by-hour insulin use, each person's insulin program can be fine-tuned and customized.

Recently, a report was published noting that the pump worked satisfactorily in eighteen patients over an average of eighteen months. No surgical or skin complications occurred, and there were no instances of ketoacidosis (seriously high blood sugar).

Dr. Jack Piotrow, the first man to have the pump implanted (in 1987), has had diabetes for thirty years. He holds the record as the longest carrier of this remarkable device. He recently said, "This pump is terrific. It gives me a handle on control that I never had with the standard therapies."

The PIMS is not considered to be a perfect solution to diabetes control. The perfect pump would, of course, completely replace the pancreas. It would have a sensor that would automatically detect changing glucose levels and release the correct amount of insulin. While scientists agree that such a "closed-loop" system is a ways off, the PIMS is a space-age step in the right direction.

Nasal Insulin Spray

A novel insulin delivery method has been developed at Beth Israel Hospital in Boston. It is a nasal insulin spray that reacts within ten minutes and lasts for about an hour, lowering the risk of low blood sugar that can occur two to three hours after taking short-acting insulin.

The commercial availability of nasal insulin depends on mixing it with a nontoxic compound that increases absorption. Scientists have recently identified compounds that are safe and effective. Several have passed FDA safety tests. One of the major drug companies is currently considering running extensive clinical trials.

The possibility of using only one injection of long-acting insulin supplemented with a nasal spray at meal and snack times is very attractive to diabetic people of all ages.

Pancreas Transplantation

Since 1966, over 2,000 pancreas transplants have been performed worldwide. The pancreas, the home of insulin-producing beta cells, is a difficult organ to harvest and transplant. Yet scientists have been making solid progress in the ways that pancreases are preserved and shipped around the country, as well as with new surgical techniques that allow doctors to graft the organ in a location where its health can be monitored.

Traditionally, these transplants have been done on patients who have had or are having a kidney transplant. But recently, pancreas transplants have been done on patients who do not need a kidney. These patients have at least one diabetic complication that is determined to be as severe as the risk of the surgery. "Surgical transplantation of the pancreas is becoming more and more a viable option for treating diabetics," says Dr. David Sutherland, a pioneer of pancreatic transplantation at the University of Minnesota.

In spite of the excitement surrounding the transplanting of this organ, there are still many drawbacks. It is a very expensive procedure involving major surgery, with the best clinical outcome (80 percent survival rate of the organ) resulting from the combined, but not simultaneous, transplant of a pancreas and kidney from the same donor. The recipient must then take immunosuppressive drugs, with their threat of serious side effects, indefinitely. Rejection is always a concern.

The positive side is that the transplanted kidney provides an early alert system, helping the transplant surgeon prescribe appropriate drugs before damage is done to the pancreas.

For patients who have end-stage complications and are receiving a kidney, the benefits are fairly easy to assess. They are released from dialysis, and they reap an injection-free life and the prevention of diabetes-induced disease in the new kidney. For patients who do not need to have a kidney transplant, the benefits do not, at present, seem to outweigh the risks of surgery, possible rejection, and lifelong immunosuppression.

Researchers are currently hard at work to find safe, immunosuppressive drugs that will make a pancreas transplant a relatively common alternative. One new drug, FK-506, is receiving hopeful attention. It is a peptide (a string of amino acids) that was originally isolated from a soil sample. Clinical trials using 111 patients, whose transplants involved heart, kidney, pancreas, and lung, have shown the drug to be effective as an immunosuppressive, and none of the patients suffered major side effects.

Several of the researchers at the University of Pittsburgh, where the trials were conducted, feel that FK-506 is "one of the most promising tools" they've seen this decade. Because of its quick success, it may be available very soon for use by transplant centers around the country.

Beta Cells to the Rescue

The word *transplant* usually brings to mind transplanting a whole organ such as the pancreas, but researchers are studying another type of transplant—a beta cell transplant, using only the insulin-producing cells. It is a surgery that is much less expensive and easier to perform than a pancreas transplant.

Of course, easier does not mean easy. Beta cell transplantation involves removing millions of tiny cells without damaging them, ridding them of harmful digestive juices that surround them, and then inserting them into another body so that they function properly.

The good news is that many of these problems are in the process of being solved. Dr. Paul Lacy and Dr. David Scharp of Washington University School of Medicine have developed a method of isolating and harvesting large numbers of islet (beta) cells. The islets they get are 80 to 95 percent pure.

Recently, they have been in the midst of clinical trials to see if transplanted islets (which contain beta cells) would produce insulin. They used a combination of islets harvested from human donors which were either fresh or had been frozen. The patients had had a kidney transplant and were already taking immunosuppressive drugs to prevent their immune systems from attacking foreign tissues. The islets were injected through the belly button into the liver under local anesthetic.

These trials have been successful. Dr. Lacy told me, "We have demonstrated that it is possible to get a patient off insulin following islet transplantation. We are very excited with these results. I am hopeful that human and animal islets, such as pig islets, can be coated and transplanted within five years."

The coating he mentions is a kind of membrane that protects the islets from rejection. There are many laboratories working to develop a membrane to prevent rejection, and Dr. Lacy feels the answer will soon be found.

There are other techniques being researched that will also help prevent rejection. One is to encapsulate beta cells in a string of sugar molecules. This sugar coating allows insulin to be secreted but prevents antibodies from reaching the transplanted cells.

Dr. Kevin Lafferty and his team at the Barbara Davis Center for Childhood Diabetes in Denver are working on another angle of the beta cell transplant issue. Dr. Lafferty's concern is that, although diabetes can be reversed in animals and people who undergo beta cell transplants, there is nothing to stop the immune system from attacking the newly transplanted cells in the same way it attacked the original cells.

In the search to understand how the islet cells are destroyed in the first place, T-cells (part of the immune system) have been cloned to be used for experiments. There is evidence that diabetes is activated when these T-cells induce inflammation around the islets. A form of oxygen is generated at the site of inflammation which is responsible for the "burn" that destroys the beta cells. Researchers have used an enzyme to, in effect, extinguish this immunological fire. This enzyme has made it possible to transplant islet cells in animals without using immunosuppressive drugs.

There is another fascinating approach that has been reported. Surgeons Clyde Barker, Ali Naji, and other members of their team at the University of Pennsylvania School of Medicine transplanted islets from one strain of rats into the thymus of another strain that was diabetic. They administered a dose of antilymphocyte serum that killed more than 90 percent of the T-cells in the recipient's body. The thymus produced new T-cells which did not attack the transplanted islets and the islets survived for the life of the rat. Ten rats were successfully treated. After the initial treatment, the rat's whole body became tolerant of the cells, and transplanted islets placed elsewhere in the rat's body were also not rejected. This success appears to herald an approach that would be applicable to other types of transplants.

Beta cell transplantation represents one of the brightest possibilities for a treatment/cure.

Complications

This section may be difficult for parents of diabetic children. It mentions many of the complications our children may someday suffer. Yet turning our heads and pretending they don't exist won't make them go away. But read on, because there is good news!

For our little ones, diabetic complications as an adult are a possibility, but not necessarily a probability. First of all, there have been many consistent indications that the better care a person with diabetes takes of himself on a daily basis, the better his chance of avoiding or prolonging the onset of diabetic complications. At the same time, there is wonderful progress being made in the treatment and prevention of many diabetic complications.

Diabetes affects practically every tissue in the body. Diabetics often develop kidney disease, nerve damage, heart disease, and/or diabetic retinopathy (eye disease). Virtually all of these problems are believed to result from the years of hyperglycemia (higher-than-normal blood sugar), and even though these problems appear in a wide variety of organs, there is a definite link to higher blood sugar.

How do elevated blood sugar levels cause damage? Research is providing evidence that there are two ways this damage happens.

The first involves biochemical pathways inside and outside of the cells. These pathways are altered when blood sugar levels increase. An example is a system called the polyol pathway. Glucose (food that's been broken down into simple sugars) is converted into sorbitol. A certain amount of sorbitol is needed by the cells. The problem is that the conversion of glucose to sorbitol is regulated by blood glucose levels. Too much glucose increases the level of sorbitol and seems to decrease levels of myoinositol, another essential chemical.

Researchers have witnessed that nerve damage in diabetic animals is associated with elevated sorbitol and reduced myoinositol levels. This defect can be prevented with drugs called aldose reductase inhibitors (ARI). Some aspects of retinopathy (eye disease) may also respond to treatment with ARIs. Because of the information gleaned from studies of the effect of ARIs in animals, researchers are testing ARIs in people and have observed some signs of regeneration in nerves that had been damaged. They are hopeful that some nerve damage may be partially reversible through the use of ARIs.

The second category involves molecules that make up the outer structure of tissues and molecules that determine gene function in diabetic cells. Higher-than-normal blood sugar can alter cells in the circulatory system by a process known as glycosylation. (It means "addition of sugar.") Glucose and other sugars become chemically attached to molecules in the body. They then undergo chemical changes, forming "advanced glycosylation end-products," or AGEs. These AGEs are dangerous chemical additions to the blood vessels that literally "gum up the works." The longer a person has diabetes, the more these mechanisms contribute to the buildup of a kind of biological "superglue."

Some of the most serious problems of diabetes are caused by the accumulation of AGEs in blood vessel walls. AGEs are very sticky, so when proteins pass through an area containing AGEs, they are often trapped. As more and more proteins get stuck, the blood vessel narrows and can't deliver oxygen as it should.

When this happens in the blood vessels of the leg, it can cause pain while walking, and if it happens in the blood vessels to the heart, it can cause a heart attack. AGEs may also play a major role in diabetic kidney disease and eye disease.

There is a drug called aminoguanidine that may allow preventive intervention in the future. In studies with rats, Dr. Michael Brownlee and his colleagues at Albert Einstein College of Medicine have shown that aminoguanidine was able to stop proteins from sticking to blood vessel walls. It is now being tested in patients with diabetic kidney disease.

Drugs such as ARIs and aminoguanidine offer a great deal of hope for preventing or reducing diabetic complications in the future. Perhaps, with individually tailored treatments and optimal blood sugar control, we can make diabetic complications a thing of the past.

PREVENTION

Now that scientists know what causes diabetes, they are experimenting with drugs that turn off the immune system so that it won't destroy the beta cells. They have found ways to intervene in the destruction of beta cells in animals and are now conducting human trials. Patients who have been given the drugs cyclosporine and prednisone entered a "honeymoon" phase in which no insulin was required. This phase lasted as long as they took the drugs.

The problem is that the drugs cyclosporine and prednisone have serious side effects that make them unacceptable for long-term use. The goal now is to find safer drugs. One drug that looks promising is Imuran.

Imuran has been used to prevent rejection in transplant patients. Using the antibody indicators mentioned earlier, doctors at the University of Florida hope to test seventy-five to eighty people who are in the very early stages of diabetes before any overt symptoms are evident. They are hopeful that it will prevent the disease from taking hold. So far, that has been the case in several patients who have avoided insulin injections for as long as five years while taking Imuran.

One young woman began to show signs of oncoming diabetes one year after her sister was diagnosed. Her doctor put her on Imuran, and her blood sugar dropped back into the normal range. It has been over five years, and she still has not had to take insulin injections.

Another possible treatment to prevent diabetes is the administration of insulin. Sounds strange, doesn't it? How could administering insulin before diabetes is diagnosed prevent it from taking hold?

Scientists have found that giving insulin to BB rats (a special species of rat which was bred so that a high percentage develops diabetes) prevents the disease for the life of the rat. The insulin therapy begins as soon as antibodies (64Ks, ICAs, and IAAs) indicating diabetes are found in the bloodstream. Researchers feel that when given the insulin, the beta cells no longer need to produce insulin. They shut down and get a rest, and the immune system no longer sees the beta cells as a target. The therapy is called "beta cell rest." Not only has the pancreas sharply reduced its insulin production during this therapy, but in addition, the proteins on the surface of the beta cells that are attacked by the immune system disappear.

A study done by diabetologists in Florida has confirmed results of a French study that showed that insulin therapy can have an impact on humans as well as rats. Recently diagnosed diabetic patients were put on a machine called a biostater, a kind of artificial pancreas, for a short period of time. It infused them with high doses of insulin, inducing a kind of honeymoon effect that spares the beta cells and allows them to gain strength. Whether the benefits will endure for more than a year with this technique is not yet known.

Whatever therapy emerges as the safest and most effective way to halt diabetes, the ability to predict the onset as early as possible and the development of safe drug and/or insulin therapies brings us closer to the day when we can stop diabetes before it begins.

THE FUTURE

Scientists once referred to diabetes as a "researcher's nightmare." It is a complex disease that has genetic, immunological, and environmental causes. Yet, they are beginning to understand this complicated disease process. For one thing, the advent of molecular biology has given them tools to investigate the immune system, and researchers are finding that basic questions being asked are common to many different diseases. Answers may come from unexpected sources.

There are already so many new drugs and treatments. Laser surgery and vitrectomy have saved the eyesight of 60 percent of the diabetic people who would otherwise be blind. Transplantation is likely to be vastly improved in the next ten years. To quote Dr. Paul Lacy, "I truly believe that we will be able to halt the progress of complications through islet cell transplantation, which will surely be well underway by the year 2000."

It's a very exciting time to be a scientist, or to be someone who has a personal stake in diabetes research. As parents, we have the most personal stake of all—the life and health of someone we love.

According to experts, there are four keys to finding a cure for diabetes by the end of this century: money, people, time, and serendipity (an openness to discovery and innovation). The single most controllable variable is money. If we can educate the public about the present cost of diabetes and the probability of curing it, perhaps the money can be raised and the atmosphere created wherein diabetes research becomes a scientific priority.

I have stressed the work and vision of the Juvenile Diabetes Foundation International. I don't mean to imply that JDF is the only diabetes organization who understands the vital importance of research. The American Diabetes Association and several regional organizations in North America are also doing wonderful work in support of diabetes research and other diabetes programs. I speak of JDF because I know its heart best of all. I present its approach as an example of what love and commitment can do. By making a cure through research a priority, we have become in only twenty years the largest voluntary organization in support of diabetes research in the world.

Now we believe we are in the final push toward our goal. I ask you to join us, or any other group, whose goal and priority is funding research. There is no greater gift we will ever give our children than the gift of good health, the end of diabetes.

Resources

ORGANIZATIONS

American Association of Diabetes Educators
100 W. Monroe
Chicago, IL 60603
1-800-832-6874
web site: www.aadenet.org
It can provide information on diabetes education programs and a
list of certified diabetes educators in your area.

American Diabetes Association
1660 Duke Street
Alexandria, VA 22314
1-800-ADA-DISC
web site: www.diabetes.org
It can provide information, educational programs, support groups,
funding for research, and summer camps. When you become a member, you automatically receive its magazine, *Diabetes Forecast,* an
excellent publication filled with the latest on diabetes.

American Dietetic Association
216 W. Jackson Blvd., Suite 800
Chicago, IL 60606-6995
312-899-0040
The voice mail system will let you order the names of qualified dietitians in your area. Press "7" to access that information.

Diabetes Treatment Centers of America
1 Burton Hills Blvd.
Nashville, TN 37215
1-800-327-DTCA
There are fiifty centers now in operation. They are all hospital affiliated
and provide the most comprehensive diabetes care available. They
also offer obstetrical and pediatric programs and support groups, and
are involved in lobbying for better protection under the law for people
with diabetes.

The Diabetes Research and Wellness Foundation
1206 Potomac St. NW
Washington, DC 20007
1-800-941-4635 (Helpline)
1-800-321-2219 (Subscriptions to the *Diabetes Wellness Letter*)
Its mission is to help find a cure for diabetes and to provide
care needed to combat its life-threatening complications. It produces
the *Diabetes Wellness Letter.* It'll be happy to send a complimentary copy.
It also has the Diabetes Wellness Network, a helpline staffed by certified diabetes educators who will answer your questions.

Joslin Diabetes Center
1 Joslin Place
Boston, MA 02215
1-800-547-5561
web site: www.joslin.org
Joslin Diabetes Center is an internationally recognized diabetes treatment, research, and education institution affiliated with Harvard Medical School. It has satellite treatment centers and affiliates across the country. It owns and operates the Elliott P. Joslin Camp for Boys and works closely with the Clara Barton Camp for girls. Joslin also publishes books, magazines, and videos.

Juvenile Diabetes Foundation International
120 Wall Street, 19th Floor
New York, NY 10005
1-800-533-2873
web site: www.jdfcure.org
JDFI is the world's leading nonprofit, nongovernmental funder of diabetes research. Founded in 1970 by parents of diabetic children, the organization's priority is to fund research to cure diabetes and its complications. Local chapters raise money, provide information, and hold meetings for parents and their children. As a member, you receive its magazine, *Countdown.* Call for the chapter nearest you.

National Diabetes Information Clearinghouse
1 Information Way
Bethesda, MD 20892-3560
301-907-8906
web site: www.niddk.nih.gov
e-mail: NDIC@info.niddk.nih.gov

The NDIC was established to increase knowledge about diabetes among patients, health professionals, and the public. It responds to requests for information and maintains an automated file of brochures, audio-visual materials, books, and other educational materials, as well as produces a bimonthly newsletter for professionals and the *Diabetes Dictionary* for patients and their families. Send a fax or e-mail to get a list of available materials.

Team of Advocates for Special Kids (TASK)
100 W. Cerritos Ave.
Anaheim, CA 92805
714-533-TASK
Trains parents to use legal means to make certain their children are afforded equal education and consideration under the law.

BOOKS, MAGAZINES, AND NEWSLETTERS

In addition to joining JDFI and ADA and receiving their excellent magazines *Countdown* and *Diabetes Forecast*, you might try the following:

Diabetes Management Services
14 Pelham Ridge Drive, Suite D
Greenville, SC 29615
1-800-367-1937
web site: www.diabetes1.com
It provides patient education with health care providers through insurance companies and it publishes the *Diabetes Messenger,* a quarterly topical newsletter.

Diabetes Wellness Letter
From the Diabetes Research and Wellness Foundation as listed on page 192.

Prana Publications
5623 Matilija Avenue
Van Nuys, CA 91401
1-800-735-7726 (Phone)
818-786-7359 (Fax)
e-mail: prana2@aol.com
For an annotated list of the latest diabetes books and audiotapes, contact Prana Publications for a complimentary copy of the *Diabetic Reader.*

VIDEOS

Parenting a Child with Diabetes, by Gloria Loring.
This video version of the book offers tips and perspectives to make living with diabetes easier. It features children and parents talking about how they cope. Send a $20 donation plus $3 for shipping to:

Juvenile Diabetes Foundation/Los Angeles
1020 S. Arroyo Parkway, Suite 200
Pasadena, CA 91105
You can also check my web site at www.glorialoring.com. My e-mail address is gloria@glorialoring.com.

Index